Katherine Barker has lived in Sherborne for many years. An historical geographer both by inclination and profession, she is a part-time tutor with the Bristol University Department of Continuing Education and the WEA. She has published a number of papers on early West Country history and archaeology and is at present chairman of Sherborne Museum, and the Dorset Museums Association.

Frontispiece
A view of The Parade that dates between 1894 (the completion of the SS Johns' Building on the corner of Half Moon Street) and 1897 (when a first floor was added to Philips and Handover, Outfitters, now Denner's).

SHERBORNE
CAMERA

Katherine Barker

THE DOVECOTE PRESS

To Emily Elizabeth and Zoë Katharine
who were born in Sherborne

1. The Conduit House from Long Street before 1883

First published in 1990 by the Dovecote Press Ltd
Stanbridge, Wimborne, Dorset BH21 4JD

Text © Katherine Barker 1990

Designed by the Dovecote Press Ltd
Photoset by The Typesetting Bureau Ltd, Wimborne, Dorset
Origination by Chroma Graphics (Overseas) Pte Ltd, Singapore
Printed by Kim Hup Lee Printing Co Pte Ltd, Singapore

British Library Catalogue in Publication Data
Sherborne camera
1. Dorset. Sherborne, history
1. Barker, Katherine
942.331

ISBN 0 -946159 -81 -5

Contents

Foreword

For some 150 years countless photographs have been taken to record people, places and events. These are valuable historical documents giving accurate pictures which bring the past alive in a wonderful way. As the pages of this beautifully produced book are turned the photographs of Victorian, Edwardian and modern Sherborne will amaze, delight and amuse. Memories will be stirred and I hope gratitude expressed to those patient photographers who took the originals and to those who have collected them so that they can be handed on to our descendants.

Katherine Barker has gathered here a representative selection from the vast archive of Sherborne photographs. This has been a formidable and time consuming task. Her work is made even more valuable by the detailed text accompanying every item. Hopefully, her hard work will be rewarded by the uncovering of photographs which still lie hidden away in albums and drawers. Sherborne Museum always welcomes copies of photographs relating to the town and the area it serves, and a selection is always on display.

We are very grateful that Katherine Barker has given us the opportunity of turning these pages to reveal Sherborne and its people photographed from the reign of Queen Victoria to the present day.

GERALD PITMAN
Vice-President Sherborne Historical Society.
Vice-Chairman Sherborne Society CPRE.

Introduction

The fascination of old photographs is enhanced when their subject is one that can be shared. Then we can enjoy, at whatever level we choose, the pleasures of the time paradox – the exploration of familiar places we know so well but which we never knew at all; a world somehow just the same and yet quite different. This is history at its most immediate and most compelling. No other medium permits us such effortless rights of trespass into the past. But as venturers in this strange place we find our experience every bit as limited as for any traveller in forbidden country, for we have no choice but to see what is presented to us. These pictures are like 'stills', single frames cut from an endless reel of a lost silent film. This is history 'framed' in more senses than one.

The Sherborne archive contains many hundreds of photographs pre-selected by the photographers themselves. Their Art was laborious and expensive and (much as today) they worked within constraints which were largely financial. They worked to commission (mostly portraiture) and for profit, concentrating on the scenic and picturesque – the proverbial 'picture postcard'. When change was rapid (demolition, for example) the appeal was immediate, but for most pictures it takes time for the 'old fashioned' to become the 'antique' and we cannot know what has been lost in the process. Medieval Sherborne monuments are well represented – but not within these pages, for it is precisely their perceived historic worth which has slowed their rate of change, and which at once makes them less interesting subjects. Sherborne Abbey looked much the same in 1860 as it does today. By the same token we are less interested in Sherbornians dressed up for their 1905 Pageant than we are in their real lives. Much more immediate are the people of the 1872 Wesleyan 'time capsule'.

It is the commonplace which is most transitory. It is the everyday which holds the attention of most of us most of the time and it is this which has influenced the choice of pictures. The captions do not constitute a 'picture-history' but have been prompted by a historical sense of place, and drawn from memories, minutes, notes and reports. Those who prefer more ordered history should refer to the work of J H P Gibb (1981), J Fowler (1951), W B Wildman (1930) and for notes on buildings to the Royal Commission volume (1952) and G H D Pitman (1983). The Abbey, Almshouse, Hospital, Post Office, Railway, Castles, Schools and Silk Mills all have their own Histories, and so has Sherborne during the Second World War. Nevertheless, there is material here not previously published, and as such is hoped to make a worthwhile – if small – contribution to the history of the town.

Sherborne's photographs take us back to 1850, the beginning of an immensely rich period which saw the making of the modern town. About half now lies beyond living memory, but it remains full of topical interest – the Town Hall Question is a case in point. Between 1850 and 1950 the population increased by only a few hundred. The principal achievement of the period was its rehousing, and one wholly ignored by the camera. Nowhere are there (surviving) pictures of the grossly overcrowded, evil-smelling slum cottage courts that characterised mid 19th century Sherborne, and neither are there pictures to be found of the social revolution that saw the successful programme of local authority house-building undertaken between 1910 and 1930. In the same way we may suspect the modern camera has largely overlooked the rapid re-population of central Sherborne, often in 'Courts' (once again), but this time for a population mostly incoming and retired.

It is not an overstatement to say that everyone who lives in Sherborne has the material for another book. There are as many histories as buildings and as many memories as people. If this book serves as a pleasurable 'aide-mémoire' for this never-to-be-written encyclopaedia, then it has done well enough. It is, perforce, a personal choice of pictures, treated from selected viewpoints. We can only ensure that our records are of sufficient quality to make possible a similar book in 2090 – should anyone still be interested. In an age pre-occupied with Historical Conservation, with the Theme Park and Heritage Business, we are reminded in these pages that the full and proper subject for photography is not the Past, but the ever-receding Present.

KATHERINE BARKER
Sherborne

Acknowledgements

In addition to works cited elsewhere, material has also been drawn from the Report to the General Board of Health on the parish of Sherborne (1850), and from 3 maps; the north Dorset manor map of about 1570, and the town maps of 1735 (1802) by John Ladd and of 1834 by Edward Percy. Unpublished sources include most notably the notebooks of A B Gourlay, the Log Book of H J Seymour, and various items in the collection of Sherborne Museum.

I am much indebted for help/loan of photographs from David Andrews, Mr A Biss, Richard and Muriel Brewer, Ted Chant, Bill Dewey, Michael John Evans, Roy Edwards, Graeme Harrison, H W F Holmes, Mrs Sybil Hunt, Mr and Mrs L R Moores, Mr R A Pitcher, Mrs Ann Smith, Mrs Pam Taylor, H L Trump, Mrs Ida Witton and to Roger Peers at the Dorset County Museum. Most of the pictures however, come from 2 large collections in the possession of Sherborne Museum and Sherborne School, without whose generous co-operation this book would not have been possible.

It remains only to thank Jim Gibb for reading the typescript and making valuable and timely comments; to Gerald Pitman whose 'Sherborne Camera' lectures are a delight to us all, for his kind Foreword; and last, but by no means least, to Emily for proof-reading, and to Zoë who finished 'A' level just in time to type the manuscript with such wit and good humour.

Photograph numbers: Mr A Biss, 121; Bill Dewey, 139, 140, 141; Dorset Natural History and Archaeological Society, Dorset County Museum, Dorchester, 63; L R Moores, 10, 47, 52, 113, 114, 157, 160; Sherborne Museum, 1, 3, 4, 8, 9, 11, 14, 22, 36, 37, 41, 43, 48, 49, 50, 51, 58, 60, 62, 65, 79, 80, 82, 83, 84, 85, 86, 97, 98, 105, 106, 108, 115, 118, 119, 120, 123, 124, 127, 131, 135, 137, 138, 142, 143, 144, 146, 150, 154, 155, 156, 158; Sherborne School, Frontispiece, 2, 5, 6, 7, 12, 13, 15, 16, 17, 18, 19, 20, 21, 23, 24, 25, 26, 27, 28, 29, 30, 31, 32, 33, 34, 35, 40, 44, 45, 46, 53, 55, 56, 57, 59, 64, 66, 67, 68, 69, 70, 71, 72, 73, 74, 75, 76, 77, 78, 87, 88, 89, 90, 91, 92, 93, 94, 95, 96, 99, 100, 101, 102, 103, 104, 107, 109, 110, 111, 112, 116, 122, 125, 126, 128, 130, 132, 133, 134, 136, 145, 147, 148, 149, 151, 152, 153; Pam Taylor, 159; Mrs Ida Witton, 38. The author, 54; publisher, 39, 42, 61, 81, 117, 129.

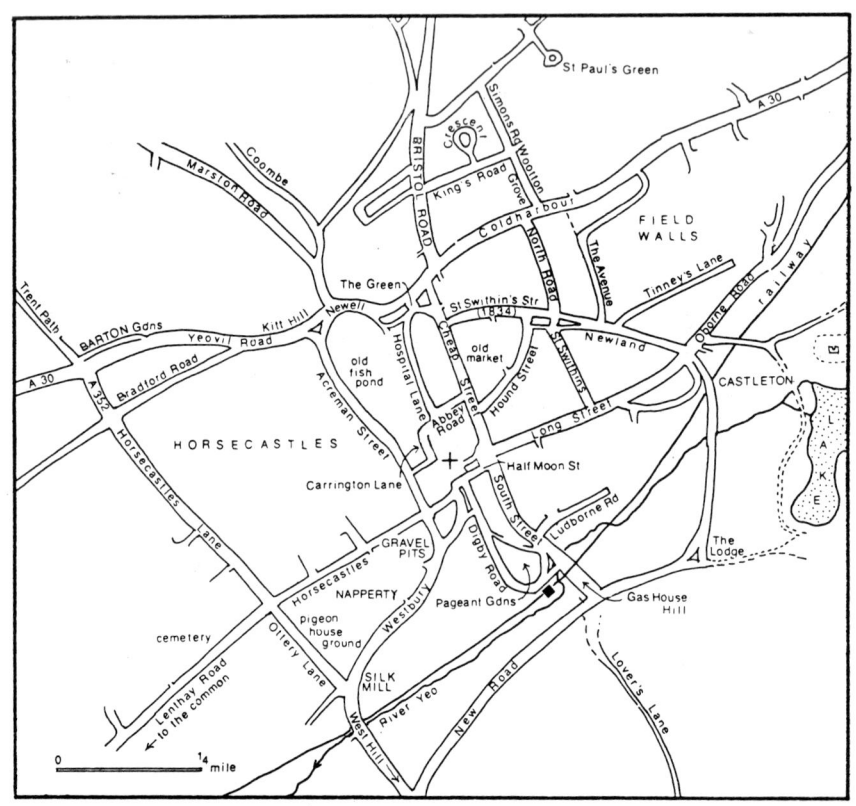

The Abbey Close

2. A unique picture, almost an aerial view, taken from the Abbey tower in 1879 by W M Chaffin who had a photographic business in Cheap Street (No 62). It is a cause for regret that this is the only (surviving) view. The countryside is very empty; no Sherborne Preparatory School (till 1885), no Half Acres, no Bradford Road houses, but cottages up the west side of Acreman Street and a cluster around Newell Grange, Horsecastles Farm and Barton Farm. The west side of Hospital Lane is empty, and it is possible to see the site of the newly filled-in ornamental pond – site of one of the medieval abbots' carp ponds. It is marked by a line of Scots Pines in the centre of the picture. The Yeatman Hospital has been open just 13 years, and the National School stands at the corner of Abbey Road newly diverted around the gate and lodge of the King's School where recent re-building can be picked out in the 'new' look of the stonework.

3. The Abbey Close during the Pageant of 1905, celebrating the 1200th anniversary of the founding of the Sherborne bishopric. The floral decoration occupies the site of the future war memorial.

The low retaining wall and railing date from 1885 but the lime trees are a great deal older. The Church Order Book of 1729 reads 'a new row of lime trees from the 'Blue Gate' (beside the Almshouse) to the church porch in the room of those now standing, and also two rows of the same trees to be planted from the said Blue Gate to the end of The Grand Jury Chamber' (the east end of the Town Hall, No 6). These trees are depicted on both 1735 and 1834 town maps; a double row to the church door and another parallel with Half Moon Street, and a single row following the lane round to the Vicarage. Only part of the Half Moon Street avenue survives; 6 trees were felled to make room for the Digby Memorial, and a further five behind the War Memorial some time after 1946.

Joseph Fowler (author of *Medieaval Sherborne*) wrote to enquire of Kew Gardens whether the limes could indeed date from the early 18th century. The answer was a definite yes, the lime is a long- lived tree, and regular pollarding, while making the trees perhaps less attractive at times, serves to further prolong their natural life-span. If, in 1729, these trees were designed to replace others, it poses the question as to who planted the earlier trees – and when.

4. 'Old buildings now a silk factory at Sherborne minster.' A very early view of the west end of the Abbey looking north over the remains of the 15th century Abbot's Hall, by this time in use as a silk mill, and shortly to be converted into the King's School Chapel. At right-angles to it and forming the rear of the Sexton's house is the former 13th century Abbot's Guesten Hall soon to be re-furbished as a large school room (the library since 1879). The dormer windows disappeared in the restoration.

The picture is from an original calotype in an album of a Mr Methuen Campbell, relative of the Mansell Talbot family, and has recently been made available by the Glamorgan County Record Office. Gerald Pitman dates the picture to about 1851; pieces of the Abbey porch can be seen ranged on the grass (restored 1849-51) and the wrought iron gateway has been propped against the wall (it was already a century old, ordered by the Vestry in 1750). The west end window of the Abbey was lowered in the 1851 restoration in which position it is shown here.

5. An engraving by Rev J L Petit of much the same view as No 4, and drawn in 1851, probably the same year as the photograph was taken. The two pictures make an interesting pair.

The cottage may have occupied the site of a side chapel of All Hallows parish church demolished between 1542 and 1550. By tradition there lived here a barber, and later a cobbler who plied his trade in the Abbey parvise (room over the porchway). By 1844 the cottage was occupied by James Coates, the Sexton, who was paid £8 a year. A second Sexton was accommodated in the parvise and his duties included those of watchman. James Coates was evicted in 1854 and compensated by the governors of the King's School. The cottage was subsequently taken down, but conditions were made that there should be no access to the churchyard from the School.

6. The earliest known photograph of the Abbey taken from the steps of the Old Town Hall, outside the 'Grand Jury Chamber' which marked the limit of the lime trees planted in 1729. The picture was taken by John Warry of Westrow House in Holwell, in 1859. He also took the picture of Newland (see No 145). The cobbles are still in place, although there is now a gravelled path laid between the avenue of trees. Even the earliest Sherborne photographs show gas street lighting; a public subscription was opened in 1832 and in 1836 an agreement with The Gas Company (see No 104) provided 161 public lamps. By 1851 there were 74 lamps recorded; the lamps repaired by the town, and the posts by The Gas Company. Sherborne Museum possesses a map of 1833 showing the earliest gas mains which were laid at least twenty years before the first sewer. The gas lamp in the picture has disappeared.

7. The Abbey from the south-west in 1866. The great restoration of the previous decade is complete but there is, as yet, no Abbey clock (set going by Mrs Digby 14 March 1874) and the tower has yet to acquire the now familiar 12 Gothic pinnacles (1884).

For centuries the ground on the south side of the Abbey had been the parish graveyard, not just for the town but for many surrounding villages – by the 1840's there were over 100 burials a year. While not as yet a danger to public health the Board of Health Report of 1850 deemed it 'highly desirable' that it be closed. In 1856 a new cemetery was opened in Lenthay.

Two years later the Abbey graveyard was levelled and about 3 feet of soil was carted to Lenthay; the bones of civil war victims were unearthed and part of the tomb stone of Abbot Clement (1155-65) removed to the north aisle. Earl Digby offered to lay out the churchyard, fell trees and re-arrange paths; new saplings protected by hurdles can be seen in the picture (although the trees do not seem to have lasted very long!). The yews were felled in 1958.

8. The Old Vicarage photographed some time before 1857 when it was demolished. The foundation stone of the present building was laid in 1857 and it was enlarged in 1878. Canon Lyon lost two children allegedly from bad drains, so the new vicarage was set back to avoid tainted ground.

The Old Vicarage dated from the 15th century and occupied the site of the palace of the Saxon bishops. The first cottage to the south (left) was built as an 18th century servants quarters; it still stands, but independent of the present vicarage.

The War Memorial

9. Peace celebrations July *1919* were unfortunately spoiled by wet weather. A procession of about a thousand strong made its way from Greenhill to the Pageant Gardens where a service of all denominations was held. Uniformed representatives at the Conduit took the salute with arms reversed.

Other events were postponed until 4 August when a large marquee was erected in the King's School Courts and between five and six hundred Servicemen and ex-Servicemen were entertained to a dinner. Sports were held in the Old Castle grounds. Over £250 was subscribed to pay for the banquet and for souvenirs for the next-of-kin of the Fallen and a further £190 was raised by a special Rate of 1½d in the £.

The War Office wrote offering the town a War Trophy – namely One German Machine Gun with Ammunition Box and Belt. The offer was accepted.

10. After the ceremony in the rain; the day has seen the unveiling of the Sherborne War Memorial, 11 November 1921. One hundred and sixty-five men are commemorated. The Half Moon Street railings have been removed to make space for the steps, but the site surrounding the memorial is not yet finished. To the left behind W Warr and Son, Ladies and Gentlemens hairdresser, is the old frontage of the Half Moon Hotel.

The cost of the memorial was £527 10s 6d. Architects fees and extras brought the total to £657 5s 6d, all of which was raised by voluntary subscription.

11. The unveiling of the Digby Memorial by Sir Richard Glyn took place on 1 July, 1885. Built in memory of George Digby Wingfield Digby . . . '[who] made it his first care to complete the restoration of the Abbey Church and after a life of generous benificence . . . loved by all classes of the community this monument is erected by public subscription 1884'. The monument was recently restored (1989) revealing anew the contrasting colours of Bath, Ham and Portland stone of which it is made. The bronze statuettes were made by Messrs Singer of Frome who cast the famous Boadicea on Westminster Bridge; they portray 4 Sherborne worthies; St Aldhelm with his harp, Bishop Roger holding a Norman church, Abbot Bradford displaying the Almshouse charter and Sir Walter Raleigh in his Tudor finery.

King's School

*Throughout this book what is known to a wider world as 'Sherborne School'
is referred to as the 'King's School', a name by which it is locally much better known.
Its historic title 'King Edward VI Free Grammar School' was amended in 1922.*

12. The south wall of the Old Headmaster's House converted from the medieval Lady Chapel in 1560. The original Royal Coat of Arms was replaced (after the Civil War) in 1660 – now replaced by a copy. Below are the Arms of principal benefactors of the King's School; Jewel (Bishop of Salisbury), Horsey, Leweston, Combe, Mullens and Thornhill, and below again are 18 sets of initials - those of the founding governors. The sundial was erected in 1745 by one Benjamin Bastard who became a school governor.

The entrance to Church Lane is marked by wrought iron gates first installed in July 1723 (and recently restored), and in Church Lane itself can be seen the 'Laundry Buildings' demolished in 1920 (see No 77).

13. The original Grammar school yard or 'School Barton'; to the left is The Old Headmaster's House. The Old School Room in the picture dates from 1606 and replaces a smaller one built shortly after the founding of the King Edward VI Grammar School in 1550. A very handsome early 17th century building, it was refurbished in 1660 when the balustrade and ornamental drain pipes were added. During the reign of Charles I the Assizes were held here, and during the Parliamentary occupation Cromwell's troops used the building as a guardroom causing considerable damage to the fabric. The bay window was not added until 1886 and lined with panelling from the old 'Sun Inn' on The Parade (just off the picture to the right).

For 300 years some fifty or sixty local boys had their lessons here, two or three teachers with six groups in the same room (the original 'open plan') working through a curriculum of Latin (including spoken Latin), Greek, Hebrew Scripture and a little Arithmetic; there was public speaking (in Latin and English) and monthly debates and plays of a suitable nature performed at the end of term. There were boarders from the beginning and in the main these were lodged with the Headmaster, sometimes thirty or more. The pump and the privies were in the yard on the other side of the Schoolroom.

14. The Old Headmaster's House before it was converted back into the Lady Chapel between 1921 and 1934. To the left just out of the picture are the steps down into Church Lane opposite the present newsagents, and to the right is the Old Schoolroom.

At the Dissolution the two chapels at this end of the Abbey were taken over by the governors of the newly founded Edward VI Grammar School, and in 1560 converted into a house for the headmaster (the date can still be seen on the wall, and is visible from Church Lane). A small oval window can be seen on the first floor; known as 'The Headmaster's Eye' it enabled an observer to watch over the goings-on in the Schoolroom! The bay window was built by Reverend Ralph Lyon in 1839, a suggestion was made that it be retained as an altar recess in the new Lady Chapel, but in the end it was removed and re-built at Sherborne Preparatory School in Acreman Street, and a new east bay added to the 13th century west bay. Lyon's son was born in the house, and in due course was ordained and subsequently became Vicar of Sherborne – a probably unique instance of a vicar born in his own church.

The house accommodated the headmaster until 1860, when Hugo Daniel Harper built a new residence, School House, in what later became known as the Sherborne School Courts (No 18). From then until 1921 The Old House served as a staff common room and lodging, and as a sanitorium for sick boys.

THE SCHOOL HOUSE EXTERIOR AS EXISTING.

AS THE LADY CHAPEL WILL APPEAR AFTER RESTORATION.

RECTORY

FORMER MONASTIC BUILDINGS NOW PART OF SCHOOL

SCHOOL BUILDINGS

NORMAN PORCH

OLD PORTION OF FRONT OF SCHOOLHOUSE TO BE RETAINED.

15TH CENTURY Fan Vaulting Continuous with Aisle

13TH Century Vaulting

CHAPEL OF ST MARY-LE-BOW

LADY CHAPEL

DARK PART INDICATES PROPOSED EXTENSION

SITE OF NEW ALTAR

15. An axiometric plan drawn in the early 1920's of the changes proposed for the east end of the Abbey – the grafting of a new Gothic-style bay onto the central medieval Lady Chapel by the architect Carroë. Three windows of the Headmaster's House were left (the present Abbey vestry). Top left is a sketch of the old frontage from the east, and top right is an artist's impression of the new frontage seen from the south-east – very close to the final, real-life appearance today.

16. *(Above left)* A room in the Old Headmaster's House (the Lady Chapel) at the turn of the century, and used by a bachelor master.

17. *(Above right)* The Drawing Room of the Old Headmaster's House (now the Lady Chapel) about 1850; the 15th century fan vault must have appealed to Victorian taste. The window overlooked the Abbey Close. The lady reading was one of Hugo Daniel Harper's 4 daughters, one of whom published her Sherborne memoirs. The partition wall was so thin the organ could clearly be heard during church services, and no one could play the piano because it disturbed the congregation.

18. School House photographed only five years or so after completion. From the time of his arrival as Headmaster in 1850, Hugo Daniel Harper resolved to build new accommodation both for headmaster and boarders. The result is seen below (the headmaster's house is obscured both by wall and trees). The foundation stone was laid on 26 June 1860 by the Earl of Shaftesbury, the great philanthropist. The boarding accommodation was for 90 boys, although there were only 40 at the time. But expansion soon followed in the wake of the railway which had arrived only a month before. (Harper was a shareholder in the railway company).

The boys are wearing top hats (abolished 1910) and the three elm trees are sole survivors of a long row of trees that once bordered a road which ran from Abbey Road to the north side of the monastery, and then into the Abbey Close. The trees are first shown on the 1735 map. They finally succumbed to Dutch Elm disease and were felled about 1978. The wall was built of the stones from The Priory which stood on the site and was demolished in 1749.

19. *(Left)* Lister Goodenough Elton Sunderland was born in 1880, and in his last year at school took up photography. This plate shows his own study. The detail is remarkable, and so is his choice of pictures, which may be compared with today's teenage tastes in wall posters. Lister Sunderland was ordained in 1905, survived the First World War and became vicar of Selborne in Hampshire.

20. *(Below)* The Day Room for the junior boys in School House built in 1860 and photographed in 1899. Purpose-built Victorian boarding school accommodation was austere; sparsely furnished, heated by coal, and lit by fish-tail gas burners first used in the school in 1841.

21. *(Above)* An aerial view of Sherborne School for Girls founded in 1899, which has been on its site in Bradford Road since 1903. The clocktower dates from 1926, designed by architect Sir Reginald Blomfield, also responsible for the main gate at the King's School. Just north of the Girls' School are the houses of Barton Gardens. In December 1919 the Urban District Council applied for a loan of £34,000 for the purchase of land on the Yeovil Road and the building of 36 houses there. In the end the whole development totalled rather more; including land, a new road, water and sewerage, the cost came to the then 'phenomenal sum' of £42,622 17s 10d (this would not now – 1990 – purchase a single house). The result was to place a 1d rate on the town for 60 years. The houses have recently been re-fenestrated but otherwise remain faithful to the original 1919 design. This picture was taken in the early 1960's when the allotments were still worked; ground since occupied by school staff houses, a sports complex and games fields.

22. *(Opposite top)* The laying of the foundation stone of the King's School Carrington Buildings dedicated to 'Arts, Science and Arms' which took place in a Masonic ceremony on 8 December 1909. The stone was laid by Lord Shaftesbury with the silver trowel used by his grandfather in 1860 (see No 18) – rescued just in time from a pawn shop. Beneath the stone is a phial of gold and silver coins and a roll book. The inscription is in Latin and it includes a bad grammatical error noticed by a junior boy minutes before the ceremony.

   In process of demolition is the corner of part of the old Abbey Silk Mill Building.

23. *(Opposite bottom)* Carrington Lane, summer 1940, the iron railings are being removed for war scrap. The Yeatman Hospital can be seen in the background.

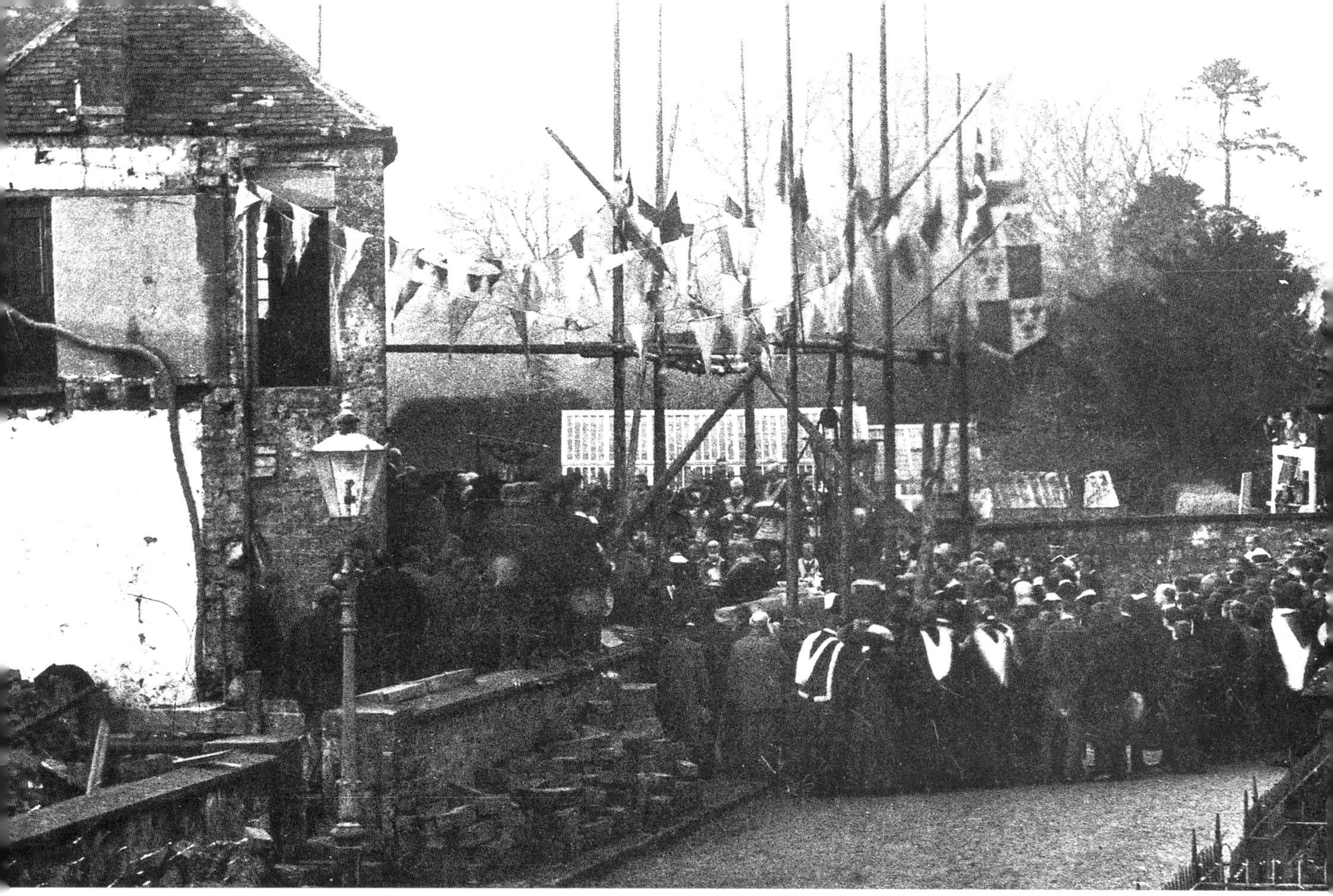

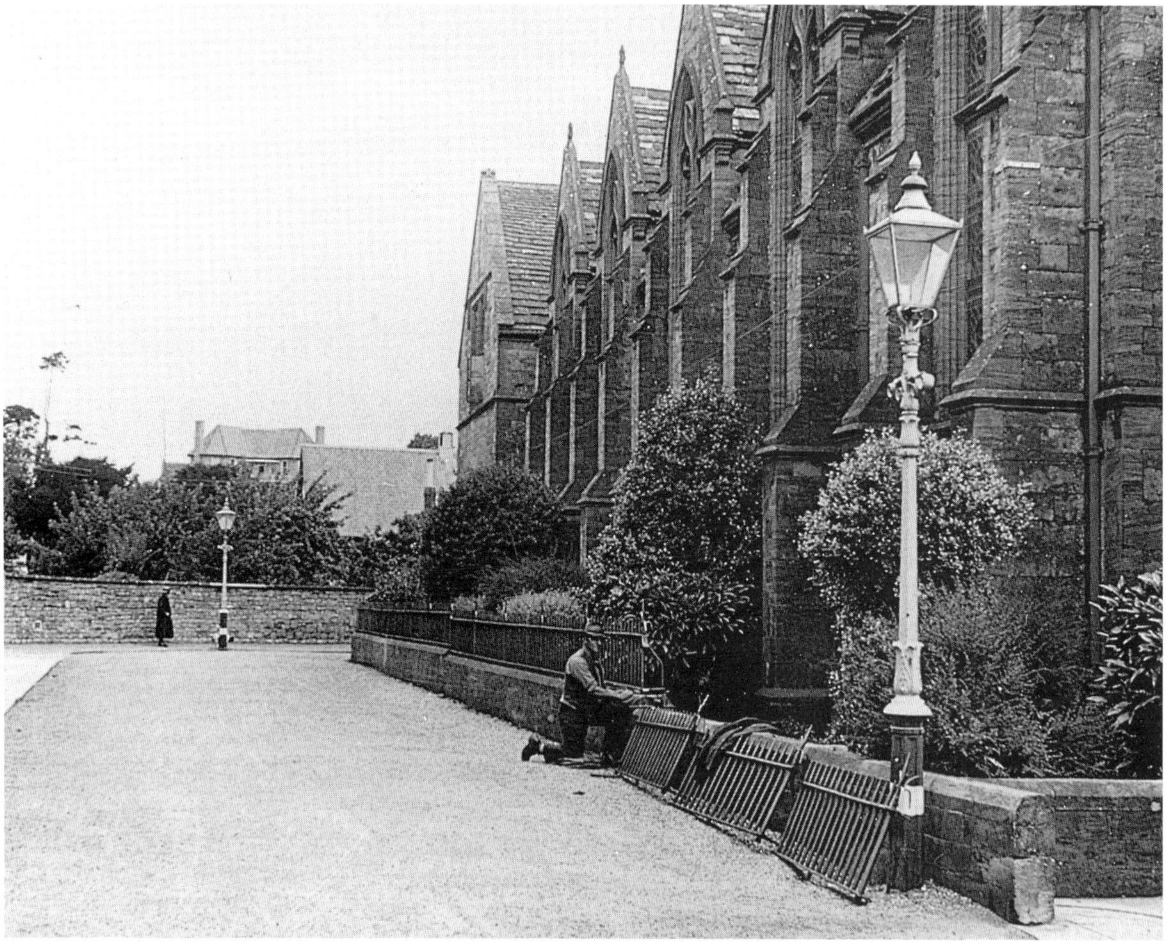

Hospital Lane

24. The Yeatman Hospital in its original form before the addition of the 3 storey wing in 1938-9. This was set at right angles to the frontage obscuring virtually the whole of the central gable, and occupying the garden where the monkey puzzle tree stands. The foundation stone was laid by Mrs Wingfield Digby on Whit Monday, 1864, in memory of Reverend Harry Farr Yeatman of Stock House. He had been chairman of The Quarter Sessions and at his death the Dorset magistrates subscribed £500 from the inhabitants of Sherborne, largely through the efforts of Reverend Harston. His children's nurse, Miss Beale, was the first matron.

25. Looking down Hospital Lane towards the Abbey some time before 1913 when the row of lime trees that can be seen across the bottom of the picture were felled for the building of new King's School classrooms. To the left is the stable and coach house of Abbey Grange, the great medieval Abbey barn which James Ridout, a King's School governor, converted into a dwelling in 1827. The cobbled pavement with the Keinton flagstones is still in existence, but the stables have long since disappeared.

26. The bottom of Hospital Lane, a view dominated today by the tower gateway of the King's School not built until 1923. At this date, about 1890, there still stands the earlier gate (later re-erected in Horsecastles) which had deflected the old course of Hospital/Abbey Lane which previously ran on directly to the north side of the Abbey. Three ancient elms remained until about 1978 as a reminder of the old line of the road (see No 18). To the left is the Lodge that still stands, and to the right one of a row of lime trees, a wall and a railing that divided an enlarged school court from the new road. The last lime was felled in 1913 to make way for a range of classrooms.

Abbot's Fishpond

27. An unpublished picture of a Sherborne garden with no obvious clues as to its whereabouts. It is in fact the site of an ornamental pond that lay at the bottom of Coombe valley between Acreman Street and Hospital Lane. The camera is pointing north towards what is now the Acreman Street carpark, and the Yeatman Hospital is just out of the picture, top right. The pillars and the dragons only date from the 1880's but they are there no longer. Does anyone know where they are?

28. There is no known photograph of the ornamental pond and this is a drawing by a Mr Bissett about 1860 recorded on a photographic plate by A B Gourlay. This pond was the last survivor of a whole series of medieval monastic carp ponds – fish for Fasts and Fridays – which at their greatest extent stretched along the valley floor the length of Hospital Lane.

   This view is taken looking south, the Abbey tower can just be seen in the distance. By 1860 so much water had been diverted the town was very anxious that this 'stagnant pest ground' should be filled in and it was blamed for an outbreak of typhoid in Acreman Street in 1867. Later the same year it was levelled – with material dug out from the new swimming bath made beside Acreman Street.

29. Wondering whether the water is warm enough, summer 1875. Local swimming places were preferably upstream of the town sewers, in Purley, at Dynney Bridge or in the sheep dip behind the old brewery. The new 50 yard 'swimming bath' was dug out in just 7 weeks and the bottom lined with stone from the Long Burton quarries which, it was discovered, tended to be both rough and slimy. There was no filter system, the pool filled naturally from the Coombe Stream culverted through an ornamental lion's head and the water was changed once a fortnight. In hot weather it was 'pea soup with water rats'.

Headmaster Harper had arranged to be the first to dive in, but he was beaten by his butler at six o'clock in the morning – before the opening ceremony. Anyone was welcome to swim for a subscription of 10s 6d a year which must have been beyond many pockets. 'Gentlemen, tradesmen and others' could swim between 6 am and 6 pm and 'respectable artisans' between 6 pm and 6 am. One wonders how many small country towns had swimming facilities by 1873 – even at a price.

It lasted just over a century. By the mid 1980's the foundation was cracked, the filtration system inadequate and the pool was emptied and a gate made into Acreman Street.

Abbey Road

30. The end of Abbey Road about 1870; the main building in the picture is 'The Abbey School for the Poor' also known as the 'National School'. In 1834 the western end of the building (left side) constituted a 'Coal Store for the Poor'. The only pupil known for certain is a G A Brine (b 1812). An intelligent but disreputable character, he ended his days in the Sherborne workhouse boasting he had seen inside every prison in England – except two.

Abbey House (to the right) was said to have been built by a Mr Simmonds, a confectioner, and in 1834 we find a Benjamin H Simmonds who owned property in Cheap Street, including a Bake House on the site of what is now Bollom's Drycleaners. In 1857 the Abbey School in Horsecastles was built and the 'National School' was used by the Sherborne Volunteers who held military parades on Lenthay Common. From 1887 both Abbey House and the 'National School' were combined as a King's School boarding house, and the latter re-built, thus taking on its present form.

Horsecastles

31. The facade of the Sherborne Union Workhouse in Horsecastles photographed in 1939 just after demolition work had started. After the original contractor defaulted the work was completed by E A Seager. Some of the faced stones were taken to the Dutch garden behind Abbey Grange. The site was levelled and almost immediately put to use as a park for military vehicles. Later it was covered by Nissen huts to accommodate American troops who supplied local children with sweets. The camp mascot, a live black bear, was tethered by a chain to a tree. Beyond the workhouse on the corner of Acreman Street are cottages pulled down during road widening in the 1960's.

32. Demolition of the Sherborne Union Workhouse is almost complete; a view taken from the workhouse garden looking north-east towards the corner of Horsecastles and Acreman Street. The year was 1939, exactly 101 years after first opening. Built to accommodate 240, the Guardian's Minute Books from 1836-1930 are in the Dorset County Record Office; on 1 April 1930 the Board of Guardians ceased to exist and the County Council assumed their responsibilities. Sherborne's first workhouse was opened in 1720 in a building called 'The Priory' that lay just north of the Abbey. This was pulled down in 1749 and the workhouse moved to the corner of Cook Lane – today a public house called 'The Digby Tap'. In 1766 one William Samson was paid £20 for serving as apothecary to the inmates of the workhouse. One medicine was 'Millipedes Wine – 2 ozs of live millipedes and 12 scruples of saffron pounded together, and a pint of generous white wine added'.

33. The Workhouse site was intended for a 'model cottage settlement' here seen under construction in 1948. A suitable name proved hard to find. First it was 'Forresters' after a Dr Forrester who had lived on the site until it was suggested that this might be interpreted as 'For Resters'. It was finally resolved to honour Councillor H Durrant who had been chairman of the UDC five times, and it remains today 'Durrants Close'.

Westbury

35. *(Below)* The photograph was taken about 1930; it will be many years before the invention of the Double Yellow Line, but a 'No Waiting' sign has already proved necessary outside the Britannia Inn in Westbury.

In the picture is the cottage once occupied by the 'Blue Charity School for Girls' today known as Lord Digby's School, founded as it was by William Lord Digby in 1743; the wall plaque just visible was put up in 1836. In the original Indenture the cottage was described as 'newly erected'. Money was made available for the tuition and clothing of 13 poor girls. The school moved across the road to Westbury House in 1887 and back again to the cottage in 1892 from whence it moved to St Swithin's Laundry in Newland (see No 138).

34. Looking south over 'Abbotty Hall' or 'Napperty' towards Westbury in the summer of 1898 by way of a long-forgotten cricket net. Sherborne's first recorded cricket match was against Shepton Mallett and was played on Lenthay Common in 1837. In 1856 the field in the picture had been rented by the King's School from a South Street butcher (just out of the picture is the 19th century Westbury slaughter house, now Tisbury Cottage). There was a cattle stall, and pond and the ground needed levelling. In 1888 the field to the right of the picture was acquired (the town side of the A 352) known as 'Pigeon House Ground' where, sure enough in 1570 we find depicted the old monastery dovecotes (or culverhouses).

To the right in the distance (with the chimney) is the 'New Silk Mill' of 1840 and just visible beyond is Riverside House, once the residence of John Sharrer, an 18th century industrialist, who so successfully introduced silk throwing here in 1753.

With the building of the railway in 1860 the course of Westbury was re-directed along its present course providing a number of houses towards the Acreman Street corner with long front gardens which they were permitted to enclose in 1863.

36. (Below) Opposite Westbury House is the Britannia Inn which, about 1910, was poised between horses and cars – 'Stabling and Motor Garage'. The archway with the room above was a fairly recent addition as can be seen from the stonework. The 'Brit' was smaller then, managed by 'The People's Refreshment House Association Ltd' of Broadway Chambers, Yetminster.

37. Wessex House in Westbury was the 'Bell Inn' in 1834 complete with stables, garden and yard. It was owned by John Mills Thorne who ran the Long Street brewery. The garden was occupied for many years by Reeves furniture shop, and latterly by the houses of Wessex Court built in 1986. During the later 19th century it was known as 'Westbury House' and both Lord Digby's School and Sherborne Preparatory School were housed there for short periods. The motor cycle works was photographed about 1930; in the picture are E Clarke, W Purchase and Reg Roberts.

38. The Church Lad's Brigade shortly before the First World War; a rather poorly preserved post card but one which shows the Rawson Hall in Westbury. The building was bought pre-fabricated 'from London' not long before by a Miss Rawson and served as, among other things, an early 'Picture Palace'. It is sited in Gravel Pits where the Digby estate had built a number of retirement homes. Earlier this corner of Westbury was known as 'Troy Town', indicative of a 'running ground' or turf maze; this area was used as play area by the boys of the charity schools in the 17th century and it was a Pack Monday fair ground at a later date.

39. In 1923 a group of Sherborne traders put up the money to form the 'Sherborne Electricity Company' and the result was Sherborne's first generating works seen here in a modern photograph (1990). It was built by Messrs Guppy & Son of Gillingham brick in what had been the gardens of numbers 1 and 2 Terrace View, Westbury. Harry Willis of Yeovil installed the engine and then stayed on as engineer-in-charge. There were two 2-cylinder and one 3-cylinder petrol and oil engines; at one end of the building was a large switchboard, and at the other was the 'battery room' where huge sulphuric acid batteries stored electricity (now the site of the SEB transformer). Everything was beautifully burnished, especially the large steel fly wheels – 'it was like a palace'.

Company representatives went out to find customers. Two meters were fitted free, one for heat (1d a unit) and the other for light (2½d a unit); for £2 15s 0d (£2.75) it was possible to have installed 3 lights and one power point. By 1929 there were complaints about the unsightliness of Sherborne's rapidly multiplying telegraph poles.

Electricity is now supplied by the National Grid. The building stood empty for a number of years until October 1984 when it was acquired by Melhuish and Saunders, building contractors, for offices and stores. It is now known as the 'Westbury Works'.

Ottery Lane

40. Ottery Lane and Horsecastles road widening in 1967, looking north to the Lenthay junction; road works before the days of orange and white cones now look curiously old-fashioned. This route once carried one of the principal routes to the north, continuing along Trent Path Lane which represents its original width. This stretch of road was 'Ottar Lane' in 1570, hence 'Ottery', but it was also once known as 'Factory Lane' linking as it did the Silk Mills with the workers' houses. The familiar 'industrial' roofscape of Digby Villas (about 1861) can be seen on the right. The uniformity of the chimney stacks was lost in the great gales of winter 1990, when the two on the lefthand (western) end were damaged and reduced in height. At the Lenthay junction there once stood the Horsecastles Toll House (its site is now a grass verge opposite 'The Skippers' public house). Sherborne's first traffic lights were installed here in 1983.

Horsecastles Lane takes its name from the fields that once stretched as far as Acreman Street (see map). *Horscastell* is mentioned in 1484, and there was also a *Horscastell Well*. In 1545 John Leland described the Conduit House as a 'fair castel'. The Conduit is well known in Sherborne but no one knows what the *Horscastell* was – except that it was for horses.

The A30

41, 42. The top photograph shows the A30 between Yeovil and Sherborne before the dual carriageway was made in 1967, the signpost stands at the Trent/Bradford Abbas crossroads. The lower photograph shows the same view today.

In 1929 there were growing complaints in Sherborne that both town and countryside were being made unsightly by the erection of telegraph poles. They are certainly a very prominent feature of both A30 photographs. They exist of course no longer – historic monuments in their own right which stood for little more than 4 decades.

43. The A30 at the top of Babylon Hill before the creation of the dual-carriageway in 1967. While certainly improved by the Turnpike engineers in the mid 18th century this was an old route that appears on a Tudor map of about 1570. The scene of a skirmish during the Civil War (between Bedford's Parliamentary forces in Yeovil and Hertford's Royalist forces at Sherborne Castle). Writers at the time called it 'Babell Hill' because it was the hill of a Great Noise.

In the bad winter of 1963 the road filled with deep drifts of snow, and traffic was frequently reduced to a single lane – if it could move at all.

44, 45. A pair of photographs of a procession making its way between Sherborne and Oborne, the caption given in a 1964 exhibition reads 'Sherborne Town Band leading Territorials to the Rifle Range (at Crackmore) about 1904'. The particular interest of the upper picture is in providing us with a view of the A30 at the turn of the century – the Tollhouse near Blackmarsh Farm can be seen on the left, while the lower one gives an excellent view of the London Train.

Yeovil & Bristol Roads

46. The Yeovil Road at Kitt Hill or Corn Hill; Newell House is on the right and the Marston Road junction is on the left beyond the cottages demolished in the 1950's. In medieval times this was Barton Cross, the heart of the manor of Sherborne Barton, the demesne farm of the monastery of which the present Barton Farm, Newell House (formerly 'Grange'), and Horsecastles Farm were all part. This was once a large open space at the cross-roads on the north-western edge of the town, an important watering place for stock (the pound was at the bottom of Marston Road). Quarry stone came this way, and Corn Hill may recall the passage of grain to the early 16th century barn that still stands behind Newell House. 'Barton barne' is marked on the Tudor Map.

Later history filled the space with Kitt Hill House and cottages (possibly the site of an old quarry), and with the cottages in the picture. The oldest house site is clearly occupied by Newell Grange, high above the road cut down with constant usage, whereas the cottages, although they may appear to be of great age, have been 'fitted in' at a later date, their doorsteps almost level with the roadway.

47. Milk delivery by horse and cart; Walter Young of the Castle Dairy, Horsecastles Farm, holds the reins at the bottom of Bristol Road. Seymours premises (with the window) still stands, but the lean-to sheds have been replaced by a grass verge. In 1834 there were five cottages here between the corner and Priestlands Lane of which traces can still be seen in the present retaining wall. The other (east) side of the road was widened in 1976 although traffic lights were not installed for another 10 years.

Marston Road

48. The Marston Road Tabernacle, the first Coombe church made redundant in 1929 with the building of a second (see No 49). It was in the days of Canon Lyon that the decision was made to build a mission church to serve the northern part of the town; a site was found, the money raised by public subscription and the church opened and dedicated on St Paul's Day, 25 January 1883. The church occupied the site of the Stoney Lane tollhouse still standing in 1850. In 1834 the Stoney Lane gates are shown extending right across this awkward junction, tolls presumably payable on both roads.

From medieval times, if not earlier, Coombe, Dymor and Redhole had been worked for local stone, quarries or 'quarrs' have left deep scars in the landscape. The last family of quarrymen in Coombe were the Mitchells who built Coombe Terrace for their workforce; but the history of the quarries is elusive and no photographs have yet been found.

49. The congregation is assembled for the laying of the foundation stone of the new Coombe Church on 26 June 1929. The first Coombe church had for various reasons become unsuitable, and for a second time a public subscription was opened. The new site was given by Lt Col J B Wingfield Digby who laid the stone, and the church was dedicated on St Paul's Day 1930. The tiled floor of the chancel and a stone tablet in the north wall commemorated Mr A Berryman who completed 29 years of Lay Readership between 1908 and 1937.

Even in 1930 Coombe Church was not well placed to serve the northern part of the town, and in 1954 it was sold and the money devoted to building a third St Paul's which opened in 1957 in St Paul's Green at the end of McCreery Road. The first St Paul's is now an antique furniture workshop, and the second, the premises of Westco Preservation Ltd.

Acreman Street

50. A lost church; the old Baptist Church in lower Acreman Street which stood on the Horsecastles corner was replaced in 1931 by a new church in North Road. The old church was then used by Messrs Bow and Osment as a workshop, until together with a row of cottages it was demolished for road widening in the 1960's. The portraits are of the first minister and his wife, Mr and Mrs Morris, taken about 1910. This church, together with the 'Tin Tabernacle' in Marston Road and the Rawson Hall in Westbury belong to the same family of late 19th century pre-fabricated buildings.

51. Acreman Street looking north before the demolition of South-Western Dairies in 1975. The houses of Acreman Court now occupy the site. Acreman Street was so-called by 1437 when it is spelled *Akermanstrete*; an *aecer-mann* was a peasant farmer, and this route led to the monastery demesne farm today represented by Barton Farm. The road was widened in 1854 when the lower part decided to abandon the name 'Cat Street'.

52. Mr Foot and his daughter with a new hand bier outside the premises of Foots Undertakers and Coach Builders at the top of Acreman Street, today occupied by Sherborne Refrigeration. One John Foot occupied a shop and dwelling house on this site in 1834, grandfather perhaps of the man in the photograph.

Newell

53. Flooding at Newell that followed the great storm of 1952, which is best remembered for the devastation of Lynmouth. Newell was in fact returning to its former state; before the Board of Health Report of 1850 and the creation of a town water and sewerage system Newell had been the site of a large and dirty pond and all traffic passed through a ford. For it was here that the Newell spring emerged, culverted by the medieval abbey from the Conduit Head in Kennel Barton (literally 'canal' of the 'home farm') which is now the Stewart Wing carpark, and flowing naturally downhill to the cloisters.

By 1834, this was the site of Mr Ffooks waterworks; the water wheel drove a single barrel pump of 3″ diameter and 8½″ stroke which made about ten strokes a minute. It supplied piped water to about 60 houses at a charge of 21s a year; the neighbouring poor had access to water at restricted times. This may be the pump we first hear about in July 1821 when to 'meet the scarcity of water on Greenhill a pump from the Newell water was supplied by means of pipes and a reservoir holding 200 hogsheads for fire purposes were supplied'.

54. The site of Mr Ffook's water wheel in 1834; a view taken in 1979 looking north across Kennel Barton to the Crown Hotel. The Coombe stream (left) has just emerged from its Victorian culvert, the Stewart Wing (opened 1973) is to the right, and in the middle distance is the wall of the car park in which a well-head can still be seen.

The importance of the spring is to be found in the name Newell, from the old English 'āewell' or ewell, source or well. It is remembered in Sherborne itself in old English scīr burn 'clear spring'. The association of an obscure female saint, Emerenciana, suggests this spring, like so many, had a pagan significance later Christianised.

The water was not so clean in 1882 when cases of enteric fever at the King's School were traced to the Kennel Barton source and the supply cut. In 1898 the King's School governors claimed ownership of the spring through a deed of 1629 and offered the town a 99 year lease at a rent. A law suit established no claim by the school. The Crown Inn appears on the 1834 map and behind it at that date was a tanyard.

55. In 1958 the wall of Newell House garden opposite the Crown Hotel was demolished and re-built on its present line (seen left of the lorry) to improve visibility on a very dangerous bend. The picture is of poor quality because, regrettably, it only survives as a newspaper cutting. The curve of the present road thus follows the curve of the old Newell House garden wall which itself replaced a one-time row of cottages demolished some time between 1735 and 1802; their foundations lie beneath the present green space, the building stone is doubtless to be found in today's wall, twice re-used.

Greenhill

56. The Horsefair on The Green about 1890, and which was to continue until shortly after the Second World War. The large open space (probably never 'green') was the site of a chapel and graveyard dedicated to St Thomas a Becket ('the Martyr') on 11 September 1177. There was also a St Thomas Fair granted to the Bishop by Henry III in 1240 – a 6 day event, it took place over the St Thomas Feast Day on 7 July.

The Green saw considerable medieval development; the New Inn (c 1480) and the 'Julian Inn' given to the Almshouse in 1437, and later the great coaching inn in the picture, 'The Angel', where by 1823 mail coaches stopped daily on their way between London, Bath and Exeter. 'Licensed to let post horses' was uncovered over the door in 1952.

At the Dissolution the proceeds of the St Thomas Fair (also known as the Green Fair, or Gooseberry Fair) went to the King's School and the Almshouse 'for the good of the town'. The Green Fair was abolished in November 1888, but the field nearby is still called 'The Fairfield' and is now awaiting development. The traffic island in the road today has its origins in a static water supply tank placed there in 1940.

57. Greenhill was improved by Edward Percy for the Turnpike Trust but the route is an old one; an alternative runs up Back Lane behind the cottages on the right, but the relative age of these 'twin' roads is difficult to determine.

The steep roads in Sherborne, especially Greenhill, were the scenes of much drunken and riotous behaviour during fairs and bank holidays (the number was reduced to 18 in 1830). But it was the night of 5 November that surpassed them all. Fire was a major risk in the days before either mains water or a fire brigade. 'The night of 5 November passed off in Sherborne fortunately without destruction of public property by fire' wrote the *Western Gazette* reporter in 1847 'but . . . we witnessed scenes of the greatest danger . . . blazing barrels filled with tar were rolling about the streets, combustible material was thrown in all directions and men in disguise were scattering lighted tar balls . . .'

Life is quieter today.

58. The committee of the Sherborne 'Bonfire Boys' in 1894; Adam Gosney, photographer and firework maker is centre stage presenting his left profile to the camera. The 'Bonfire Boys' were, in effect, the carnival committee and the Lions Club rolled into one. From 1876 they organised the events that accompanied the 5 November celebrations. These centred round a lengthy carnival procession – torch-lit after dark – which always took place on or about Guy Fawkes Night, indeed, Mr Guy Fawkes sometimes presided.

Sherborne Museum has a collection of 'Bonfire Boys' posters – wordy, witty, featuring and making light of burning local issues. Sometimes the national scene intruded – the 1887 Jubilee, Zeppelins, the Rates(!) and the National Strike were all used as carnival themes. The last 2 posters are dated 1934 and 1936, and they have a curiously modern ring. The theme was the 'Pool for Youth' – there was a strong feeling that young people in Sherborne needed more facilities and a swimming pool was high on the list. Purley had been put forward as a suitable site and a fund opened. There the archive stops.

Cheap Street

59. Sherborne Fire Brigade coming down Cheap Street resplendent in red and gold during the Jubilee Procession of 1897. Not until 1863 were the first steps taken in the formation of a proper fire brigade. The first uniform – with the helmets – dates from 1877.

In 1720 we learn that fire appliances were kept in the Abbey (in the north choir aisle), and consisted of 4 ladders, 2 crocks and 32 buckets. The Sexton had the job of ringing the fire bell and churchwardens were empowered to provide a hogshead of beer to encourage would-be fire fighters. It was the boys of the King's School who provided such 'excellent services' in this respect and would rush out at the sound of the bell 'to form the lines'. In 1870 the boys got to a fire in Horsecastles actually before the Sexton rang the bell. The latter resigned in a fit of bad temper and after that it was the duty of the parish clerk who was henceforward paid 2s 6d a year for his trouble.

Headmaster Harper's daughter recalls . . . 'we well remember Papa going off with the boys to put out fires and bringing them back to have hot brandy and water before they went to bed. Fires occurred regularly every winter . . . the fire bell was very ancient . . . it was turned inwards at the bottom and gave an awful reverberating sound . . . in the middle of the night it was terrifying.'

The first steam appliance was introduced in May 1921 – the end of hand pumping and free beer!

60. Mould and Edwards in Cheap Street, now occupied by Olivers, which has retained some of the 1926 shop fittings. The photograph dates from 1921 before the creation of the archway that now leads to the Somerfield supermarket. In 1926 Ralph Hunt of Blackmarsh Farm decided to develop his dairy business and needed access to the area behind Mould and Edwards premises for a milk factory. An archway was created, exactly the width of the shop living room, and the frontage re-designed. To the left was a lock-up shop (now Sherborne Photographic) and to the right a well-equipped grocery and butchers shop (now Olivers).

For many years milk lorries coped with a works entrance only just wide enough (the wall still bears the scars). Hunts Dairies closed in 1986, the factory was pulled down and the archway now opens onto an attractive pedestrian precinct.

In the picture are Roy Edwards in Fosters School uniform (his father was out buying eggs that morning) with assistants Messrs Kendall and Elmley.

61. The archway from Cheap Street to the Somerfield supermarket as it appears in 1990. It was created by Ralph Hunt who, in 1926 needed access to his new dairy business behind what was then Mould and Edwards (see No 60). The frontages of both Sherborne Photographic and Olivers date from that time – the smaller archway originally formed the doorway to the left-hand shop.

62. Cheap Street looking south from Chaffin's Studios in 1903, which is today the Southern Gas Showrooms. W M Chaffin started his photographic business in 1856 and several of the early pictures in this book are attributable to him. This part of Cheap Street was more residential than it is today, conspicuous by their absence are the shop fronts of Dodge and Son on either side of the street.

Cheap Street follows an ancient north-south route that crosses the river Yeo near the present railway crossing, traversing the New Road it continues on up Lover's Lane deeply incised with centuries of traffic to the top of Gainsborough Hill from where it can be traced today in a green road. The other north-south route lay over West Bridge and up Watery Lane – the present West Hill dates from 1848.

63. Cheap Street before it was made one-way; road works are in progress early one morning about 1930. The bay window over the Swan Inn (now The Swan Gallery) has been removed long since.

64. *(Right)* Flower Show banner in Cheap Street put up in the summer of 1888; Mrs Leah Hunt is standing outside Kingdon's on the corner of Hound Street (see No 136). There have been changes to almost every frontage in the street; Trasks (on the site of Boots) was a publisher of some note. A maid holding a duster leans out of a window above what is now Constance Wood, and the man holding his lapels is John Dean, a gardener. The road is very dirty, and the pavements worn and uneven.

Flower shows were a great feature of Sherborne life from 1861 until they were abandoned in 1891 because of financial losses. Held every year in August in the grounds of the Old Castle they were preceded by a colourful procession to the Abbey. Apart from the many horticultural entries, there were stalls and sideshows, military bands and marquees, boating on the lake and fireworks designed and organised by Adam Gosney (see No 89).

65. *(Below)* The premises of what is now 'Lo-cost' supermarket in Cheap Street as it appeared shortly before demolition in the mid 1930's. Both to left and right the frontages have changed very little, but Lo-cost is unrecognisable. The attractive late 16th century doorway was lost in 1937 when the premises was completely re-built by F W Woolworth. While the foundations were being dug 'a line of orderly burials' was found at the rear of the former premises. Nine burials were recorded by Charles Bean, including 2 children, but an eye-witness report recalls many more. The age of the cemetery is not established.

The shop in the picture is empty awaiting its fate, but for nearly 50 years it had been the premises of Sidney (later Charles) Stagg 'Practical Boot and Shoe Maker'. The Staggs also ran a small lending library – 4d a book' (see No 59).

66. *(Left)* Undated but early view of what is now Dewhurst's the butchers (70 Cheap Street) during restoration. Plaster has been stripped off to reveal the gable end of a probably Elizabethan jettied half- timbered building, square panelled with decorative members at the corners, giving a distinctive diamond pattern. The relation with the building to the right is not established but it is possible they once formed a single unit, an end hall (Dewhursts) with a domestic range attached, similar in plan to 'The Julian' at the top of Cheap Street.

The camera has just caught the words 'SAVINGS BANK' over the doorway of the fine neo-classical building to the left, probably the original premises of the Sherborne Bank which opened in 1818. The upper room was the meeting place of the Masonic Lodge of Benevolence also founded in the same year, a delightful room with a blue ceiling painted with gold stars. It is today the premises of Southern Electricity.

68. *(Following page)* The Parade in the mid 1920's; 'F Bennett & Co Ltd., Printer' is mounted over what is now the 'upper' part of the Abbey Book Shop. For the first ten years of its life this building seems to have housed a single shop (an ironmonger) and then in 1852 it was divided into two. In 1989 the shops were re-combined and the frontage completely re-designed. A tiled floor reading 'Bennett's Library' was re-laid in the new central doorway. A printer had operated from this building at least from 1862, and Bennett was only one of several. The business finally ceased in 1987 when the last printer removed to Priestlands Lane.

67. *(Below)* The bottom end of Cheap Street between 1889 and 1893; the Conduit House has just been moved back to its present position although the gas company has not yet moved the lamp post which remains 'stranded' in the road. The Conduit was restored at one and the same time and some stones from the old Lady Chapel incorporated into the structure. However by 1889 the Conduit's useful days were largely over. In 1861 it had been rented by the Rev Harston at £1 a year for use as a penny bank, and in 1870 it had been used as a depot for the reception of articles for the sick and wounded of the Franco-Prussian war. The railings were finally removed in 1872 and an animal drinking trough placed on the side nearest the road in 1882. This survived until 1987 when a drunken driver crashed his car and badly damaged it.

Sawtell's the butchers is on the Long Street corner where now stands the Midland Bank, and beyond is Adams Clockmakers shop. Denners (as it now is) in South Street has no second storey. The gates of the old shambles (meat market) on this site were re-used as the South Street entrance to the Pageant Gardens in 1906; they were removed during the Second World War and in 1980 were duly replaced by the gates of Elmdene (Wallace House) following the widening of the house driveway into South Street.

69. It is a quarter to nine on a sunny morning in Cheap Street about the year 1855. A breeze has lifted the sun screens on the windows of what is today the Abbey Bookshop, a building then little more than ten years old. The photographic detail is good enough to show a pavement of cobbles and flagstones on the other side of the road; the only one now surviving is in Hospital Lane. Behind the Conduit is a pair of shops and a tall three-storeyed building which were all demolished in 1893. Beyond can just be discerned the then very narrow entrance into Half Moon Street and beyond again the canopies of two market stalls occupying the site of today's Denners.

About 1735 the medieval market cross was removed from this corner, and the Old Crown Inn demolished. The site was cleared and later bought by Earl Digby who built 'The Shambles' (meat market) to replace the one near the Conduit which he intended to enclose for the sale of vegetables only. By 1866 a letter to the local newspaper lamented the poor condition of the market and recommended demolishing The Shambles and sweeping away poor 'Old Joe's coffee shop' in Market Street (South Street). But The Shambles lasted until 1870 when a single storey drapers store was built (Denners). An echo of the Old Shambles survives today in the disused abattoir behind the premises on the Long Street-South Street corner.

71. *(Right)* The oldest known photograph of the Conduit House dating from about 1850; the damage is on the original 6" glass plate. The Conduit has glazed windows and is surrounded by a high railing put there in 1844 to protect the reading room and library which had cost the town £140 to equip. Further security proved necessary, but only three years later the whole idea was given up when someone stole the lead from the roof! By 1851 it had become a police station (a pound for drunks). The people in the photograph are difficult to see, but one is wearing a top hat, and two are in smocks. An early gas lantern hangs above the fountain from which flows a constant stream of water which seems to run away into a gulley behind the raised kerb of the roadway. This is the Newell source piped (in a 'conduit') to the Parade where the Conduit House was moved from the cloisters about 1560. In 1850 it was still an essential clean water supply; there were only five other pumps in the town and well water was often suspect.

In February 1833 a service of thanksgiving had been held for protection from cholera; that summer the poor were employed making an underground drain for taking the filth away from Cheap Street. If the photographer had moved his equipment into Half Moon Street he would have been able to record for us the stagnant open sewer – but not the smell.

In August 1850 members of the Vestry decided not to implement the Public Health Act, a regular water and sewerage system would be too expensive. Fortunately for the inhabitants of Sherborne they were overruled.

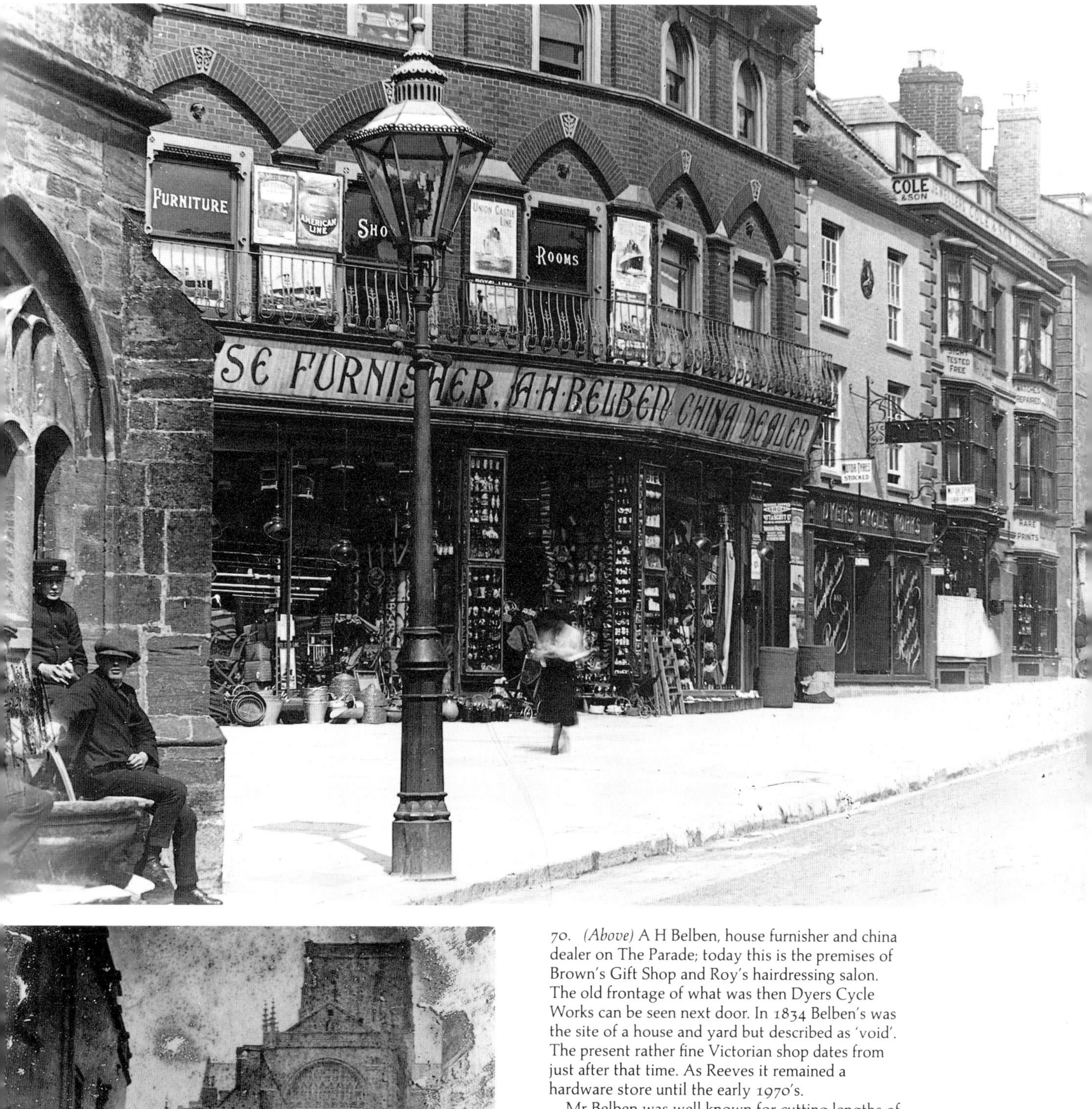

70. *(Above)* A H Belben, house furnisher and china dealer on The Parade; today this is the premises of Brown's Gift Shop and Roy's hairdressing salon. The old frontage of what was then Dyers Cycle Works can be seen next door. In 1834 Belben's was the site of a house and yard but described as 'void'. The present rather fine Victorian shop dates from just after that time. As Reeves it remained a hardware store until the early 1970's.

Mr Belben was well known for cutting lengths of lino (linoleum) on the pavement in front of his shop. (*Linoleum*, a hard-wearing floor covering that served much the same purpose as modern vinyl.) Sometime before the First World War, Mr Belben built six houses in Bristol Road opposite Priestlands (then open land used for trench digging practise in 1914). His only stipulation was the initials of the house names should spell BELBEN – and they still do – *B*uena Vista, *E*lmwood, *L*yndhurst, *B*racknell, *E*pworth and *N*etherleigh.

72. The Conduit House looking east from Abbey Gate before it was set back from the road in its present position (1889). Curiously, no photographs of the move survive. To the left is Penny's Ironmonger, and to the right a jewellers shop demolished in the road widening of 1893. The figures standing round probably include Josh, Jack and Dan who would carry luggage to and from the Station for a small consideration. The Parade was re-surfaced with Keinton Mandeville flagstones in 1846 and it is shown here drying after rain. It was not re-surfaced until the early 1970's.

73. The Sun Inn on The Parade in 1901; by this date the rendering had been removed revealing a fine half-timbered building. The Sun Inn was known locally as little more than a 'doss-house' – tramps and others could spend a night by the fire for just 2d (less than 1p) and if they wanted a bed it would cost them 4d.

   To the right is Humphries Cycle Shop and the Cross Keys Hotel. The focus is so sharp the posters can be read. The King (Edward VII) wants recruits (for the Boer War), Mr Lemare is giving two grand organ recitals at the Congregational Chapel in Yeovil, and there is to be a Sherborne Horse Show on 25 July on Lenthay Common. Throughout the 18th and 19th centuries the Common was the site of horse racing, 'cudgelling' and 'single stick' and the 'annual diversions' in August attracted large crowds including gentry.

74. By the time of the First World War the Sun Inn had been taken over by W A Dewey who had a total of 85 men billetted with him. After the war it re-opened as a 'Temperance Hotel' with 20 bedrooms. The rent and rates were precisely £1 a week. Dewey's was known for its 'Stodgers' – a half pound of bun dough with currants and sultanas which cost 7 for 6d (2½p). The second and subsequent days the 'Stodgers' needed toasting, – thereafter they were known as 'Gut scrapers'.

Early in the 1920's W A Dewey moved to what is now Dewhursts (see No 68) where he also set up a motor taxi service, which also transported school children – probably the first schools bus service in the county.

5. *(Below)* Abbey Gate, once the south-eastern entrance to the medieval monastery and where John Cutler (born 1766) remembered a massive oak gate' in his boyhood days. Several Yeovil men were hanged here after the Battle of Sedgemoor in 1685 and their remains dismembered and put on display. To the left of the arch is a doorway into Abbey Gate House (probably the site of a postern gate). In the centre of the lane is an open drain (now covered) and to the right, under the arch is 'Sansomes Hotel'. The picture was taken before 1880 when the archway coping was repaired.

76. *(Below)* A post 1880 view of Abbey Gate; the door of Gartell's China Shop is open for business. The last of the family Miss Albertina Gartell was killed in the air raid on Sherborne in September 1940. The doorway had gone by 1900, improvements to Abbey Gate House seem to have followed the reconstruction of the Half Moon Street corner in 1894.

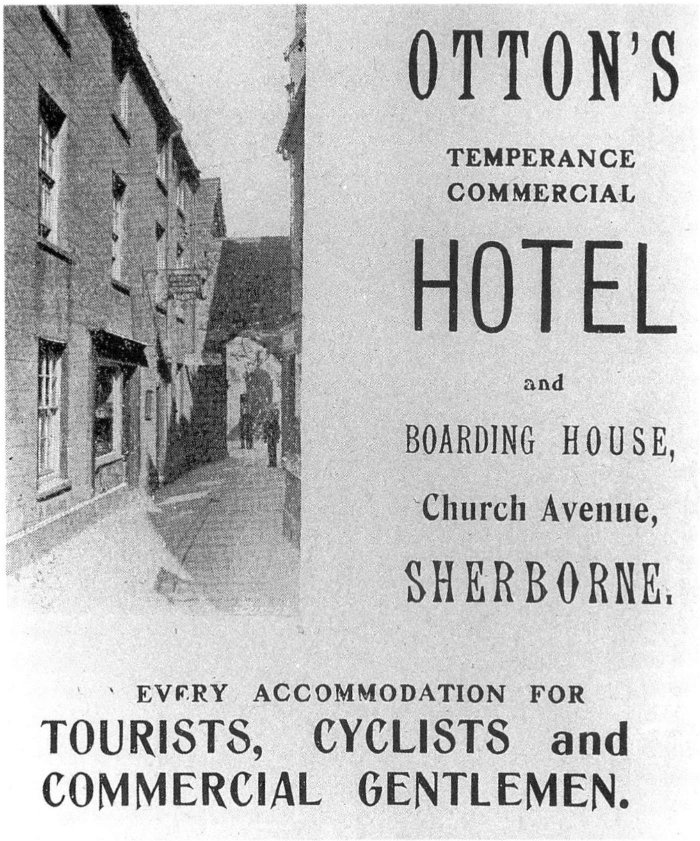

OTTON'S

TEMPERANCE
COMMERCIAL

HOTEL

and

BOARDING HOUSE,

Church Avenue,

SHERBORNE.

EVERY ACCOMMODATION FOR

**TOURISTS, CYCLISTS and
COMMERCIAL GENTLEMEN.**

77. *(Left)* Looking towards the Abbey Gate and The Parade; to the right (just outside the picture) is Abbey Gate House, now Sherborne Museum, and to the left is 'Otton's Hotel' demolished in 1920. Formerly known as the 'Laundry Buildings' it was purchased by Reverend Ralph Lyon (headmaster of the King's School 1823-45) as boarding accommodation; by 1850 it was in a very poor state and was sold, only to be re-purchased by the King's School (together with the Sun Inn) and sold a second time in 1892. It then became successively Sansomes Hotel, Stagg's Temperance Hotel, and Otton's and served as a soup kitchen during the First World War. Purchased a third time by the King's School in 1916 it was pulled down in 1920 to give better access to the old Sun Inn - now Bow House.

78. *(Below)* In 1834 one Richard Tuffin owned a bakehouse and shop on the corner of the Abbey Close and Church Lane; from 1801 Tuffins had been something of an institution as confectioner and 'tuck-shop' especially to the boys of the King's School across the lane. 'Dear old Miss Tuffin, with her corkscrew ringlets . . . early in my first term I was sent to buy . . . twenty penny worth of pink pigeons milk . . . the dear lady took pity on an innocent child and thus began a friendship that lasted many years'. The corner was completely rebuilt in 1900 and is now Macnally's newsagents. Only two cast-iron bollards remain.

79. The Methodist Church (formerly the Wesleyan Chapel) in Cheap Street was built largely through the inspired efforts of William Dingley who arrived in Sherborne from Cornwall in 1821 to set up a drapers business. He laid the foundation stone on 23 June 1841, galleries were added in 1862 and a polygonal apse added in his memory in 1884. The original chapel cost £1887 13s 10d.

CLUBS
and
CHARITIES
SUPPLIED.

Best Value
Possible
for
Ready Money
Only.

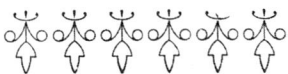

80. *(Above)* Until 1851 the Methodist (Wesleyan) Church had no entrance from Cheap Street. In that year 'old buildings' were taken down and a pair of new shops erected on either side of a wrought-iron gateway at a cost of just £130. It is interesting to note that in 1834 the dwelling house and garden here (forming the future site of the shops, gate and graveyard) had belonged to William Dingley himself who presumably sold them to his fellow Wesleyans. It was the time of the Health Report and we may imagine Dingley taking this opportunity to 'improve' his property.

In 1903 the left-hand (the lower) of the pair of shops seen here was the 'Bon Marche' now Gillards Tobacconist. The other shop, W H Newcombe Watchmaker, was once identical, but was badly damaged in the air raid on Sherborne in 1940 and the window was replaced and the gable removed. Together they form an interesting example of a complementary pair of mid-19th century purpose-built shops, and must have been among the first to enjoy mains water.

81. *(Right)* Numbers 54 and 56 Cheap Street as they are today; built in 1851 as an identical pair of shops, number 54 (W H Newcombe) suffered damage in the air raid of September 1940 and was partly re-built.

Those that seek Me early shall find Me

Looking unto

82. *(Above)* Members of the Wesleyan Guild in the Wesleyan Sunday Schoolroom about 1900 (now the Powell Theatre). The church had been built with only limited space for a schoolroom and by 1870 it had become inadequate. A garden was purchased in Abbey Road alongside the church and a large new building was put up at a cost of £1419, the architect was a Mr Lauder of Barnstaple. It consisted of a large central room 59' high, 2 large classrooms, a boardroom, library, 'convenient offices' and separate yards for boys and girls. There was provision for gas heating and a boiler for tea meetings. By 1870 Wesleyans were playing a very important part in local education; their Sunday School pupil roll stood at 500, of which some 200 were adult.

The Schoolroom was re-opened as the Powell Hall (after Robert Powell, headmaster 1950-70) by Sir Richard Luce Minister for the Arts on 11 March 1986 and has full theatre and lecture facilities. Curiously, it does not seem to be the first theatre in Abbey Road; in March 1831 two plays were performed at 'The Theatre, Abbey Road'.

83. *(Left)* A close-up view of the 'time capsule' unearthed from beneath the foundation stone of the Wesleyan Sunday Schoolroom in 1985; the 2 portraits are of Mrs 'J E Dingley April 1872' and 'Rev James Smeeth'. There were a further 29 in the bottle, a number taken either by Adam Gosney or by William Chaffin in their local studios. In addition there were newspapers, programmes and an account sheet. The stone was laid on 1 May 1872 by T F C May with a solid silver trowel with an ivory handle given by Messrs Harding and Cole (see plate 101), who also made the arrangements for the bottle. Following the stone laying there was a tea party, and then an evening meeting in the Chapel when a further £350 was promised on top of the £1000 already raised. It is impossible to calculate what this would mean in current prices, but must be worth at least ten times that amount, and probably very much more.

84. William (left) and Samuel Dingley from their photographs which were placed in the Wesleyan Schoolroom 'time capsule'. William is wearing the white necktie 'a mark to know a Wesleyan by' as he remarked in his opening speech at the 'elegant luncheon' he gave at the Digby Hotel in 1872 to celebrate his 50 years in Sherborne. It was an occasion that immediately preceded the stone-laying ceremony in Abbey Road during which the 'time capsule' was placed in the wall.

Established nearly 70 years.

COLE & SON,

THE PARADE, SHERBORNE.

WATCHMAKERS, JEWELLERS, OPTICIANS, ENGRAVERS, DEALERS IN ANTIQUES.

Rare Prints.

Miniatures.

Silver.

China.

Sheffield Plate, AND Furniture MAKE OUR OLD ROOMS AND GALLERY WORTH A VISIT.

SOLE AGENTS FOR **GOSS.**

85. John Coles ran a Manufacturing Watchmakers and Silversmiths on The Parade, and it was he and Rev Richard Harding who made the arrangements for the 'time capsule', the bottle and its contents buried under the foundation stone of the new Wesleyan Schoolroom in Abbey Road in May 1872.

Their photographs were placed in the bottle with 29 others, together with a brochure detailing the goods and services offered by Cole's shops in both Sherborne and Weymouth. In addition to optical instruments, barometers and time pieces of every possible shape and size, he sold jewellery – 'Portland pebble and Seaweed Brooches', 'Pebble, Jet and Hair Bracelets' and 'Hair alberts in gold and plated mounts'. He made church clocks to order and he could provide a 'Stout- cased Horizontal Watch suitable for a Working Man' for exactly £3. At Pack Monday fair in 1989, the author bought a man's watch for almost the same price.

The photograph of the shop dates from 1903, by which time Cole and Son have added 'Old Rooms' and a 'Gallery' full of furniture and rare prints. For many years the shop has been Edith Anderson, Ladies fashions, and has recently reopened as Fantasia.

86. John Cole (left) and Rev Richard Harding, the former photographed in Sherborne, the latter in Ventnor, Isle of White, both portraits found in the Wesleyan Schoolroom 'time capsule' for which they were jointly responsible.

Half Moon Street

87. Residents of the Almshouse return from their Devotions in the Abbey as they had done, and continue to do, since the foundation of the House in 1437. The foundation deed provides for 12 men and 4 women – all to be 'poor, feeble and ympotent'. The building (probably occupying the site of an earlier almshouse) consisted of a chapel and a hall with dormitories above reached by an external stair. The kitchen and privies were emptied by the Coombe Stream which ran under the Chapel and was accessible by way of 2 trap doors either side of the communion rail. The Almshouse charity was maintained through rents, and it became a significant property owner (96 houses in Sherborne by 1834). The Brethren together with the Governors of the King's School (often one and the same body of men) played a major part in the government of the town.

The residents are wearing their uniform; the men in caped coats and shovel hats, and the women are in scarlet cloaks and poke bonnets. They are entering the gate and cloisters of the Victorian wing of the house designed by William Slater in 1864. The uniform was modified in the 1930's, and has now gone out of use, although the men continued in the old style until the mid 1960's.

88. A rather poor photograph that shows a funeral procession on its way to Lenthay cemetery passing Vincents grocery store, 'The Supply Store', at the corner of Digby Road and Half Moon Street. There was a shop here in 1834 but the building was completely re-modelled following the opening of Digby Road in 1860. Later Carter's Stores, it re-opened as Sherborne's first supermarket about 1961; the ground-floor windows were re-designed but the first floor remained unchanged. Succeeded by a Spar supermarket, and then by Gateway, trading finally ceased on 31 March 1990 and the site scheduled for re-development.

There is no record as to whose funeral cortège this was, though it is clearly that of a prominent local citizen. It was photographed, we imagine, by Adam Gosney, whose shop can be seen on the extreme left-hand side of the picture.

89. In 1897 Adam Gosney, photographer extraordinary, took this picture of his own shop beautifully decorated for the Diamond Jubilee. Today it is better known as the premises of C B Brett and Son and 'Graphic Examples'. Gosney was a man of great talent but minimal education. Originally employed at The King's School as a boot man, he picked up photography by doing work for the boys. Eventually he had twenty-five caravans travelling the West Country engaged in photographic contract work; one of these caravans lay for many years behind Kingston House in Long Street. But sadly, he never made his fortune. The Pageant of 1905 nearly ruined him. He laid in a great stock of pictures, but things were not so organised that he could easily sell them – the train times allowed visitors little time to buy souvenirs. He was left with a huge unsold stock, some of which is in the Museum, which is regularly offered further copies of the same pictures – in mint condition.

90. The Town Hall just before demolition in 1884; the view was taken from Digby Road. The hall had been built to house the assizes and provide a covered market; the money was raised by public subscription and Dr Nathaniel Highmore (celebrated physician and warden/governor of the King's School) was appointed treasurer. Having set up the library at the King's School he turned his attention to the Town Hall which was completed in 1681. On the 1735 map it is the 'Town Hall and Market House' and it was here the 'Grand Jury Chamber' was situated; the last session of the county assizes was held in 1824.

The building was the focus of town life for two hundred years; here proclamations were made, dinners were held, Friendly Societies met, there were public meetings, lectures and assemblies. In 1821 at a farewell dinner for the Rev John Cutler, sixty persons ate venison given by Lord Digby, and a 'Champagne Dejeuner' was held in 1850 to celebrate the tercentenary of the King Edward Grammar School. In 1851 the Vestry handed over much of its power to the new Board of Health which held its first meeting in the Town Hall. As a building however, it was no longer large enough, it seated only 200 people. After very considerable deliberation it was decided to pull it down with a view to building another bigger and better place of assembly.

91. At the end of its life the Town Hall had an air of dereliction and was clearly in need of restoration! The quality of the plate is such that the notices can be read. Over the door is affixed 'Working Mens Reading and Coffee rooms'. There were cottages for sale, and a lecture given by Mr J P Uran; higher on the wall in an earlier hand it reads 'Stick no Bills Here' once behind the lamp post, and a second time beside the door. High on the wall is a list of market tolls, fees payable according to the animal, and defaulters faced prosecution. The market closed promptly at half past ten. On the extreme lef-hand side of the photo there is a public urinal; two similar 'splash-backs' still survive, one at The Julian, and another outside The Old Mermaid in South Street – both beside former market places, respectively The Green and the Shambles.

92. The Town Hall during demolition (1883-4); something of the structure of this 17th century public building can be seen, but the arms on the pediment are too worn to read. The oak floor went to the King's School library and the stone was re-used in the Abbey tower and in the building of Cricket View in Westbury. Many bones were found when the ground was levelled.

The discovery of bones is a reminder that Half Moon Street is the result of 12th century planning. Between 1122 and 1139 Bishop Roger made a new road by cutting off a piece of the graveyard on the south side of the church for the benefit of people going to the 'iter publicum' which we may take as Long Street. It is unlikely there was no earlier route along the south side of the church, but he probably effected some useful road widening.

93. Bow Passage pictured from Half Moon Street. By 1840 the building with the double bow window 'Ye Central Coffee Palace' had been the Sherborne Stamp Office where W S Penny advertised the sale of new paper, envelopes and 'labels' (ie the new postage stamp – the 'penny black'). By 1885 the post office had moved to 67 Cheap Street, but the 'Coffee Palace' still retained a 'Dickensian sub-post office with a sideline in canes to beat the boys'. The proprietor of the Coffee Palace was W Green, a specialist in Banbury Cakes and curing warts which he did without touching, 'just give me a halfpenny'. The building was demolished in 1893 and completely rebuilt (now the premises of Bath Travel) but there remains today a GPO Pillar Box in the corner by the Church House.

94. Does anyone know where this is – or was? A hitherto unpublished photograph of an unidentified Sherborne 'office' it is to be found among A B Gourlay's collection of glass plates and labelled simply 'Ceiling – Long Street?' A number of early plates were taken of buildings immediately prior to demolition and it seems likely this room has either disappeared or changed beyond recognition.

The pictures on the walls are of local views (the abbey is post-1884). There are bundles of papers and parcels untidily piled on the counter and there are articles which clearly needed weighing. There are small sorting boxes on the right-hand wall. Possible candidates include a bank, stamp or post office – possibly even the old sub post office demolished on the corner of Half Moon Street in 1893.

Note. While correcting the proofs of this book the author chanced to visit 'Tudor Rose' in Long Street. Here, probably, is the room in the photograph.

95. 'Bow Passage', the archway which once linked the Parade with Half Moon Street was 'a great place for lovers and people in a hurry'. It was demolished, together with the buildings to its left, in 1893 (see No 96). A pump is clearly visible, and notices in the rear windows of the old Post Office read 'This establishment is closed, sale on Thursday next'. Completely re-furbished it is now the Sherborne Conservative Club, the first and second floor windows remain, but the entrance was re-designed.

96. By the end of the 19th century the extreme narrowness of Cheap Street-Half Moon Street corner had led to a number of accidents, traffic having considerably increased following the opening of the railway. A particularly bad accident in which a man driving a butcher's cart was thrown from his vehicle and smashed his skull on the kerb stone prompted the Quarter Sessions of 1891 to order the demolition of the buildings on the corner, and the widening of the road.

The Conduit had already been moved back to its present position in 1889 and Messrs Adams and Penny's shops were removed in 1893. The operations were in charge of Mr Betten, a local builder. The figure at the top of the ladder is likely to be Robert Adams (the occupier) and his daughter Carrie peeps round the door. At the foot of the ladder are William Pope and Tom Dewfall; the splendid figure with the white beard is Alfred Crocker. Known as 'Ffooks Folly' in life, under demolition the corner became 'The Ruins'. The total cost was £822.

97. A further view of demolition work in 1893 at the corner of Half Moon Street and Cheap Street, this time taken from the (single storey) roof of what is now Denners. Bow passage is open to the sky (bottom right) and the door and windows of The Cross Keys Hotel can be seen beyond (top right). 'Ye Central Coffee Palace' has been taken down and workmen have reached the back wall of what is now the Conservative Club. The main part of this structure was left standing and 'made good' but with the addition of a number of features including a new doorway and a 17th century overmantel said to have been brought from 'The Julian' at the top of Cheap Street. To the left has been exposed the yard of Abbey Gate House (now the Museum) which was also due for some major improvements.

98. A closer view of Half Moon Street corner in mid-winter of 1881; the narrowness of the old corner is exaggerated by the snow drifts. There are two butcher's shops on the right (the open meat market or shambles stood on the corner of South Street until 1870), but the angle of the camera makes it difficult to see the entrance into Long Street. The drum clock stands at about twelve minutes to six; on a winter's night it would have been dark, and we can only wonder if it had been affected by the blizzard and stopped!

99. Half Moon Street looking east before 1884; on the left is the Town Hall and on the right is the 'Kings Arms, Family, Commercial and Posting House'. In the 1755 Turnpike Act it seems to have been the starting point of the road to Bishop's Caundle, by way of Gainsborough Hill. An earlier 'Kings Head' was located on the north side of Greenhill. Beyond is the Plume of Feathers (named after the badge of Henry, Prince of Wales, lord of the manor 1610-12) part of which was then a pork butchers shop. Beyond again, the hanging kettle betokens Bannister's Ironmongers; the shop front is still in place today.

On the other side of the road the Town Hall almost obscures its precursor from view – the old Church House. Completed by about 1534 the ground floor provided space for shops, and the upper floor for meetings and assemblies.

Standing in the street are the respective shop proprietors; on the left outside the post office (with the bow window) is a postman – possibly John Penney postmaster 1860-80. A former pupil of the Kings School he lived on until 1915.

100. The south side of Half Moon Street showing the frontage of the old Half Moon Hotel; to its left is J. Cross, Ironmonger (The House of Steps). In 1936 the proprietors of the Half Moon purchased Dingleys with a view to building a new hotel. Thus it is the present hotel is set back from the road, and Sherborne has its only example of 'Stockbroker Tudor' architecture. The foundations of Dingleys are beneath the present forecourt.

Mr Dingley described the street as it was in 1850 . . . 'There is no sewer whatever, the only drainage from [the houses] is in a small gutter 12" - 15" below the surface; this . . . goes through the premises of William and Samuel Dingley and at certain times the stench is intolerable . . . the gutter empties itself into an open drain leading through the Half Moon premises (the archway can be seen in the picture) and goes out into the field . . .'

In 1735 Half Moon Street was called simply 'Lodborne' and South (Market or Duck) Street was 'Lodborne Lane'. 'Borne' means stream, and 'lod' comes from a word meaning culvert or drain. In 1950, roadworks in South Street uncovered a fine stone culvert some 6' wide and 4' high – the origin of the medieval name of 'Lodborne' perhaps. By 1850 an open drain that ran down the centre of the street (foul with slaughter house rubbish) was meant to be flushed out daily by the 'pond in the Abbey' but it rarely happened as it should. This may have been the drain that was the subject of a law suit in 1463.

101. The Dining Room of the old Half Moon Hotel as it was between 1923 (electric light) and demolition in 1936. On the tables Colman's mustard and Lea and Perrin's Sauce betray the kind of menu on offer, and glass tumblers hold little promise of a wine list.

102. *(Above)* Chennell the Saddler's Shop in Half Moon Street, and over the shop (to the right) the premises of 'Senior Goodwin and Young, Auctioneers, valuers and land and estate agents'. Chennell's was sited between the old Half Moon Hotel and William Dingley's drapers shop, and was destroyed by a direct hit during the air raid on Sherborne 30 September 1940. Henry Ireland the shopkeeper was killed outright. The site was cleared and never rebuilt; it remains today the open space between Denners and The Half Moon Hotel.

103. *(Left)* South Street taken at the same time as No 100; Frisby's boot and shoe shop is visible in both. Harden Trevett's Hardware Stores is already on the telephone and the world seems full of errand boys bicycles, and hand carts. Harden Trevett & Son supplied the man-hole cover in the Almshouse courtyard.

Digby Road

104. On 23 January 1934 the great Wolsey bell returned from re-casting at the Whitechapel Foundry and was hauled from the railway station by Kings School Boys. With the bells out of action, townspeople were surprised to hear the New Year of 1934 'rung in'. A gramophone and 2 amplifiers fixed to the Abbey tower produced a noise level that could be heard at Oborne!

In the background beyond the Police Station is the distinctive form of the Gas Works. The year 1823 is the first mention of gas street lighting, but not unitl 1836 was a rate levied 'under the provision of Lord Portman's Act' to light the town by arrangement with the Gas Company. By 1850 there were 74 lamps and they were lit between October and April. The biggest problem was vandalism. Interestingly enough, the Gas Works were situated near the Railway Station, but well before the railway was even contemplated. Radstock coal, at least 800 tons a year, was all hauled by waggon. A Gas House, Boardroom and Offices were built in 1863, which remain but rather altered. The Gas Works were closed in 1957.

105. In 1910 a crowd gathered to watch the laying of the foundation stone of the Digby Memorial Hall in Digby Road. From the time of the Town Hall demolition, plans were in hand to build a new and better place of assembly. The death of G D Wingfield Digby in 1883 (the same year) had however delayed matters, postponed again with the death five years later of J D Wingfield Digby. In 1904 with the death of J K D Wingfield Digby the decision was finally made to build a memorial hall, which it was still hoped, might offer the town the same rights and facilities as a Town Hall.

106. The Old Police Station and Court House first opened in 1858 in Digby Road – a new road not fully in use until the completion of the railway station in 1860. From 1842 under the Parish Constables Act an unpaid resident was nominated annually to perform necessary police duties. In 1847 the Vestry appointed three paid constables, but not until 1857 were plans made for a properly equipped building which cost the then very considerable sum of £1692 5s 9d. This building was pulled down in 1964 and until the new station on the same site was ready Court sittings were held at the Manor House and the police operated from the Westbury Hall. The new station was opened by Hon Sir John Stephenson, a Judge of the High Court of Justice on 22 September 1969. The total cost of the new buildings was £53,976.

37. The Digby Hotel as it appeared shortly after opening on Pack Monday, 11 October 1869. Digby Road is newly embanked forming causeway across low-lying land (Half Moon Meadow) to the railway station (1860).

This rather 'upmarket' Railway Hotel was built (so it is said) as the result of a wager by George Digby. The architects were Messrs Carpenter and Slater (who played an important part in the 19th century restoration of, respectively, the Abbey and Almshouse). A large assembly room was added in 1878, well patronised after the loss of the Town Hall ten years later. In March 1875 the inaugural meeting of the Dorset Natural History and Antiquarian Field Club [Archaeological Society] was held here and it remained the Society's head-quarters for a number of years.

The hotel was run as a family business until 1900 by which time it was proving so expensive it was sold to the Saunders family who still operate a garage and car-sales business from the old stable block.

Some of the evergreen shrubs planted in the ornamental garden are still in place and grown into sizeable trees; the lower part of the garden is now Bradford's. The Hotel was bought by the King's School in 1962 and converted into a boarding house.

The Railway

108. Navvies working on the railway line at Milborne Wick about 1858; the first sod was cut with a silver spade at Gillingham in 1856. The line was first open to Sherborne on 7 May 1860, to Yeovil on 1 June, and to Exeter on 19 July. The Milborne cutting is 1 in 80 – the steepest gradient on the line. Sparks from labouring engines making the ascent frequently set light to the embankment.

   Newspapers of the day report a number of accidents during construction work. One man fell into the Castleton mill weir and nearly drowned, and another carrying a box of gunpowder under his arm lit a match . . .

09. Sherborne railway station was opened on 7 May 1860 amid great festivities; at 6.30 am as the first train left for London 1200 children were massed on The Slopes to sing 'God Save the Queen' and a cannon fired from Dancing Hill. Flags flew, the Abbey bells rung, and at 10 o'clock Divine Service was celebrated by Reverend E Harston whose sermon was preached to the text 'Many shall run to and fro, and knowledge shall increase'.

The first public meeting to discuss the formation of a Salisbury and Yeovil Railway was held in the Town Hall on 26 March 1846, but differences of opinion about the gauge, the route, and problems raising the necessary capital delayed the scheme by several years. The proposal of 1856 had been for a route north of the town, along what is now Kings Road and Priestlands, crossing Coombe by a viaduct, and rejoining the present line by way of Bradford Road. In 1857 powers were obtained to deviate at Sherborne to a straighter course. By this time there was a new owner of Sherborne Castle who unlike his predecessor, had no objection to the railway so near his residence, but stipulated that two fast trains a day should always stop at Sherborne.

10. A passenger's view of Sherborne Station in the 1860's; there is no footbridge (1886), signalling is rudimentary, ballast covers the tracks and the 'up' platform is very short. The men in the picture are probably station staff. Train services were 4 a day each way, and 2 on Sundays. The fastest took 4 hours and 2 minutes to London, and cheap excursions were available on the 12.45 train at 12s (60p) 1st class, and 8s (40p) 2nd class or covered carriage. Not only was rail travel incredibly fast, it was cheap. A journey to London by mail coach took 12 hours, and riding 'inside' cost well in excess of £3.

The first derailment at the station was in March 1879, and the first recorded accident was about 1890 when a man left the 'up' train and walked behind the last coach straight into the path of the 'down' train. A paperboy on the platform at the time tells the story 'what with the sight of the poor man's brains dashed all over the ground I could carry no papers that day . . .'

111. Castleton before the railway, the picture was taken before engineering work had started, but the wall knocked down on the extreme right may suggest surveying had already begun. Thus the most likely date for the picture is the winter of 1858.

The track was to run along the foot of the churchyard wall (through the line of washing!) straight through the large house in the centre of the picture, then the row of cottages to the right, and on through East Mill, all of which were demolished. Waterloo Terrace in Oborne Road was built to accommodate local people made homeless.

Castleton was a medieval borough with two mills, a court leet, a market and annual fair that grew up at a crossroads outside the main gate of the Bishop's 12th century Castle. It was bypassed first by the New Road (1852) and then finally and irrevocably by the railway. Unitl 1894 Castleton constituted its own very small parish entirely surrounded by Sherborne. Since 1894 the reverse has been the case – Sherborne surrounded by Castleton!

112. 'The 3.44 up' wrote A B Gourlay as a caption for this plate. The photograph was taken with the intention of 'matching' the view of 1858; they make an interesting pair – before and after the railway. Diesel replaced steam on this line in 1967.

New Road

113. Mr Grayer, the groom, in the Squire's Carriage in the New Road, parked on the wrong side! New Road was not very old when the picture was taken. In 1852 Earl Digby gave notice that he intended to stop Park Road and Snakey or Sneakey Lane and to substitute a new public highway from the Black Horse to Dancing Hill (see map). The parish won public access to the upper part of the field called 'Clay Pits' to be laid out, and planted and supplied with seats, and a footpath across Purley. The upkeep of the road was to be the responsibility of Earl Digby. The photograph shows the cobbled surface of what is likely to be the original pavement; the iron railings that bordered the original road are still in place, although the seats have been replaced. The present Lodge and gates date from this time.

114. Charlie Childs with his sister Jane at the wheel (Sherborne's first woman driver?) seated in a 1914/1915 French De Broun wagonette, ouside the Lodge in New Road. The registration is the familiar FX for Dorset, and it was the 186th car. It was Edwin Childs who first started a motor business in Long Street (in the premises of what was, until recently, The Bike Shop) and it was about the time of this photograph he moved along the street and took vacant possession of what is still known as Childs garage.

The car in the photograph was sold to Reg Hawkins at Ilchester and for a long time remained on display at Cheddar Motor Museum until it was sold to an American buyer.

South Street & Ludbourne Road

115. Flooding at the bottom of South Street in 1979; the river Yeo has burst its banks and canoeing was made possible between the platforms of the railway station. Just out of view to the left of the picture was the site of the Middle Silk Mill. With the building of the railway the mill was demolished, the mill pond filled in and the river canalised. In 1735 this was Melmoth's Mill. Melmoth waxed rich and built Grosvenor House in Horsecastles (now Westcott House) but he set up an educational charity for local boys he took on as weaving apprentices. In the 12th century it was St Andrew's Mill when so far as we know, it ground corn. Thus from the 12th century if not earlier, this part of South Street was occupied properly and intentionally by a large, well managed millpond. In 1890 it made a re-appearance and the bridge was widened. With the development of the lower part of the town flooding has become less than welcome and the 1980's saw a major flood relief scheme undertaken.

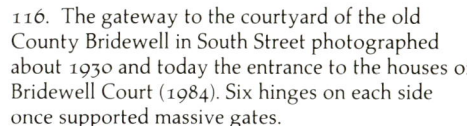

116. The gateway to the courtyard of the old County Bridewell in South Street photographed about 1930 and today the entrance to the houses of Bridewell Court (1984). Six hinges on each side once supported massive gates.

This was Dorset's 'House of Correction' or Bridewell (after the gaol near St Bride's Well in London). Here two prisoners died of 'cold and want' in the harsh winter of 1763. In 1793 it was closed and the inmates moved to the new County Gaol in Dorchester and the building sold. It then served as a brewery, and by 1834 it was occupied by John Penny, proprietor of the 'Sherborne Journal' whose offices were a few doors up the street in a long-lost building that stood in the present front garden of Wallace House. The old Bridewell, it seems, was his printing works. By the time of the photograph part of the Bridewell served as a garage and filling station.

117. A present day view (1990) of part of Ludbourne Road. In 1909 the Urban District Council (which took over from the old Board of Health in 1894) purchased Ludbourne House ('Hall') and garden with a view to building a new and much-needed Town Hall in what was to become Ludbourne Road. The same year however, a Digby Memorial Hall was proposed, and the Town Hall never happened. Ludbourne Hall remained UDC offices for many years, moving to the Manor House in 1948.

The Council subsequently decided to develop Ludbourne Road for housing and in 1912 Messrs Guppy & Son tendered to erect 25 small and six large houses. This created a road through what had once been an ornamental garden and out along a field wall that bordered the edge of the river meadow. These houses were inspected in 1913 by the Sanitary Inspectors who reported them 'the best planned and constructed cottages and far in advance of any in the west of England at a similar cost'.

Long Street

118. H Durrant, grocer, with his staff at the corner of Long Street, about 1910. H Durrant was chairman of the Urban District Council five times in 1910, 1919, and 1924-6, and Durrant's Close in Horsecastles is named after him. In the Cheap Street window of his shop is an advertising slogan which reads 'DON'T GO TO BED' but the second line is indecipherable!

119, 120. Two views of the end of Long Street, the photograph on the left taken during the Abbey restoration of 1979, and the other taken about 1900. There have been considerable changes on the north side of the street.

Long Street has been 'long' since at least 1437. For many centuries travellers have followed a 'scenic' route that takes them straight to the Abbey Church. This is unlikely to be the result of chance, and more likely to reflect medieval planning. The indications are that at some early date the western end of an already existing route was re-directed so as to lead through the south-east precinct gate into the monastery.

121. Shorts, the grocers shop in Long Street where 'Jon of Mayfair' and 'Floral Design' now stand; the frontage has been rebuilt. The picture was taken in 1902 or 1903. Standing at the door are Mr A Biss, grocer, and Tom Woods who was taken on as apprentice in 1902. In his first year he earned 3/6 a week (17½p), in his second 4/6 (22½p) and in his third, the princely sum of 5/6 (27½p). He left with a good reference in 1906. There are tins of Macfarlane Lang biscuits beside the door, but on special offer was tea a 1/8 a pound (about 8½p) and two qualities of currants – the more expensive was 4d a pound (less than 2p).

122. Long Street before 1872; there is no Abbey clock, no tower pinnacles and the Conduit is still surrounded by a high railing. On the right is Adam Gosney's first shop (he moved to Half Moon Street about 1879), the building still stands but the bay window has been removed. Beyond are the gates of 'The Retreat' (now Harper House) and on again are the cottages that occupy the site of what will be Child's garage. Just visible at the end of the cottages is the ornamental gate to two more fine gardens which belonged to the houses on the south side of the street, now Old Bank House and Abbot's Litten. The cottages on the left were rebuilt and set back in the 1960's.

123. *(Above)* The workers at the Long Street Brewery taken by Adam Gosney probably about 1870; at that date he had his photographic shop just over the road (see No 122). Photography was new but Gosney clearly possessed a great sense of history. For this is not formal portraiture, the men are not pictured in their Sunday Best but in their ordinary working clothes and accompanied by the tools of their trade. To the left are two 'white collar' workers and to the right, in his frock coat and top hat is the boss.

124. *(Left)* A wider view of the yard taken about 1920 in which the brewery workers were posed. The Dorsetshire Brewery (Sherborne) Ltd was established in 1796 and known towards the end of its days as 'Baxter's'. In 1834 it was 'Thorne's' owned by John Mills Thorne who also had possession of (among others) the Castle Inn at the end of the street. A century earlier a single large building of similar plan occupied the site and the brewery of 1796 may have been a re-founding of an earlier establishment.

John's brother Benjamin, owned a fine 18th century house almost opposite the Brewery, now called 'Thorn Bank'. The brothers Thorne were in fact proprietors of a bank – several bank notes still survive.

A good water supply is essential to brewing. In 1850 the premises are described as 'Mr Ffooks Brewery' – the man who owned Sherborne's only waterworks. No pump or well is marked within the Brewery in 1850, but a large open water course flowed out from the boundary wall of the works down to the river, running along what is today the eastern edge of Culverhayes carpark.

Derelict for many years, the building was re-developed between 1983 and 1986 as high quality apartments and maisonettes now known as 'The Maltings'.

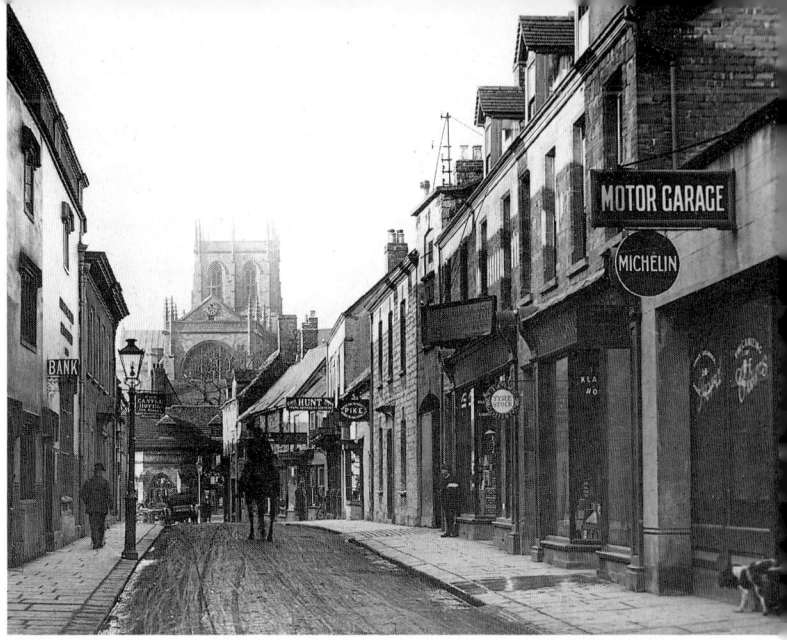

125. *(Above)* 'THESE GATES PILLARS FOR SALE' – a notice has been posted on the gates at the entrance to Harper House drive in Long Street. Situated in Hound Street this handsome 18th century house, known as 'The Retreat' until 1910 was formerly Digby property. In 1873 it was rented by the King's School as boarding accommodation and the housemaster and his family enjoyed a large ornamental garden. Sometime between 1835 and 1850 several cottages were acquired and removed, and an imposing entrance created in Long Street of which this is the only known photograph.

In the 1890's Reverend J Blanch was housemaster. Giving pursuit one night to his daughter's lover, the young man ran down the long drive and (finding the gates locked at the bottom?) hastily climbed a tree and refused to come down. This was a great scandal at the time. What became of the unhappy pair history does not record but about 1896 Reverend Blanch sold the garden in response, it is said, to financial worries, and the trees were felled and the gates no longer needed. But the entrance-way still remains – on the east side of Child's garage giving access to a private carpark.

126. *(Above)* Long Street about 1920, the entrance to the pleasure garden has disappeared and been replaced by Sherborne's first motor garage (dogs are not a new problem!). 'Sherborne and District Cooperative Society' is now the China Gallery. On the roof above is early telephone equipment; the first exchange was in Trendle Street but by about 1910 it was taken over by the GPO.

127. *(Below)* The Red House Long Street about 1890, two groups of children are posed rather uneasily for the camera, and a maid in a cap peeps from an upstair window. In the garden a lady is watering the flowers, a gardener is hoeing and a boy is standing with a basket.

The history of this house is obscure; it was built in the late 17th century and completely faced with brick about 1730 when the forecourt was laid out. The house has a very distinctive plan which is easily identified on the town map of 1834, but not in 1733 when there is a row of properties shown here along the edge of the street. The porch in the photograph no longer exists.

128. The corner of Long Street and South Street was completely re-developed in 1926 when the timbers of a 16th century shop front were exposed and preserved and complete with plaque can be seen to the present day. They were found behind the frontage to the left of 'C D Parsons Licensed Dealer in Game' where the Midland Bank now stands. The wrought ironwork can be compared with that of another corner shop, McGann's Bookseller and Stationer (see No 136) between Hound Street and Cheap Street, both of very similar style, and both products of another re-development a century or so earlier. Both corners were Almshouse property in 1850 and their history could doubtless be traced. Neither was a shop in 1834, and at this date the Long Street corner was the residence of two brothers, Edward Thomas and William John Percy, the former a land surveyor and architect who was responsible for the 1834 map and terrier, copies of which are in the Museum.

It is late in the afternoon and Mr Parsons has sold out and cleared his window. 'Special today' included Cod 8d (about 3p), Plaice 1s (5p), Rock Salmon 6½d (2½p), and 'Lobsters from 1s'.

129. *(Below)* Aerial view of the area between Long Street and Hound Street taken in 1975, a recent picture but one that already records many changes. The houses of St Swithin's Close are occupied, but heavy machinery is still clearing The Wilderness site, and the remains of Wilderness House itself are still visible. It had been built by Col Baxter who owned the Long Street Brewery in its later days. The Brewery itself is still semi-derelict and had been in use as a cheese store. A Nissen hut occupies part of the garden site of the new houses below Digby Hall carpark. The Old Market carpark is established, the Swan Yard has just been opened up for shops (1975) and heavy lorries can be seen parking outside Hunts Dairies. The factory itself is just off the picture but some of the subsidiary buildings can be seen, the foundations of which now lie beneath the Somerfield carpark.

The Digby Hall (1972) was built in what had been, until 1966, the Sherborne sheep market; cattle were sold in the 'Old Market' although in 1834 these fields are simply 'paddocks'. At this date both the Digby Hall area and Fosters school and yard formed a single field (a continuous wall can be seen in the photograph) then simply known as the 'Fair Field'. There is no knowing how old this name might be, but an association with the medieval St Swithin's Fair seems likely. In 1834 the market was certainly thriving - 5000 sheep and 200 bullocks were sold and wool sellers 'obtained 20d a pound'.

The Pageant Gardens

130. The new bandstand in the Pageant Gardens has been set up for the first public demonstration of the phonograph – and Dame Nellie Melba is to sing. The bandstand had been given by Edward Dingley, and the chairs by people who performed in the Pageant; these alas, were sold off by the Town Council in the mid 1970's.

    Sherborne Museum possesses the Pageant Garden accounts for 1906, the year it was first laid out. There were 24 men employed, they worked a full 6-day week, 10 hours a day, and were paid on average, 2s 8d a week. Stone breaking at Kennel Barton paid slightly better. Three of the 24 men were unable to write their names, and placed a mark to record receipt of wages.

131. Sherborne Military Band in the old Half Moon Field or Meadow before the laying-out of the Pageant Gardens in 1906. Sammy Beaton is the conductor and concerts were given on Thursday evenings throughout the summer months. This bandstand is not the one seen in No 132 and seems to be an earlier structure. The field could be marshy, and it is on record that bandsmen used planks to keep their feet dry! (There are planks under the stand.) In the background is Ludbourne Hall – still a private house.

2. Money raised by the Pageant in 1905 went towards the laying-out of a formal garden in what had been the old Half Moon Field
en in the picture. This had been the Pack Monday fairground (until 1820 it had been in the Abbey graveyard, and then Gravel Pits). The
reground looks well enough but the ground tended to be very marshy and planks had to be laid for bandsmen to approach the stand.
here roundabouts were set up tons of clinker had to be brought from the Gas Works to secure a firm foundation. The field was given by
B Wingfield Digby on his coming-of-age, and the Pageant Gardens were opened on 5 September 1906. Pack Monday fair was
nceforward held on the Fairfield in Coldharbour.

3. 'This year' wrote a Sherborne diarist in 1905 'will always be remembered for 'The Mother of Pageants' held in the Old Castle
rounds under the Master, Mr Louis Napoleon Parker'. Designed to celebrate the 1200th anniversary of the founding of the town and
shopric in 705 it was 'attended by thousands from all parts of the world' who assembled to enjoy a series of 'Episodes' in the history of
e town performed by local people – not unlike the 'Community Plays' that have been such a feature of Dorset life in the 1980's.
ozens of costumes were made, music was written and the text fully published. The impact was clearly enormous in the days before film
d television and gives us an insight into the way Edwardian England saw its history. The 'romantic ruins' of the Old Castle before
storation made a wonderfully evocative setting. The picture is of the final tableau.

Hound Street

134. The old Foster's Schoolroom and Boarding House in Hound Street at the turn of the century. The town map of 1735 marks the 'House in which Foster's School is held' in the Abbey Close; endowed originally by Richard Foster in 1682 it was known as 'The Blue Coat School'. The School was in effect re-founded in the 1870's by the appropriation of ten Sherborne charities. In 1875 a new schoolroom was built in a field adjoining Hound Street known as the 'Fair Field' and in 1887 the governors were able to build a boarding house to accommodate both boys and headmaster. Taken over by the County Council in 1938 a new school was built in Tinneys Lane. The Hound Street buildings have been empty since 1988.

135. Cottages in Hound Street before demolition in 1964; the line of the pavement remains but the new houses were set back from the road. The far house (towards Cheap Street) was occupied by Walter Penny, Carpenter and Undertaker; the large gates gave access to his workshop and yard. Mrs Minnie Hann lived in the house nearest the camera. Her husband was the first man in Sherborne killed in the First World War.

The Hound Street cottages were already Digby estate property in 1733, and those in the picture have the distinctive Digby emblem on their number plates – an ostrich with a horse shoe in its beak. Hound Street was mentioned in the Almshouse Subscription List of 1437; 'Hound' because of its sinuous course perhaps – bent like a dog's tail.

136. *(Above)* McGann's Bookseller and Stationer on the corner of Hound Street and Cheap Street about 1920 and which is now Barclay's Bank. The shop windows are lit by handsome gas lamp brackets, and full of the most wonderful bric-a-brac; pictures, cards, dolls, games, and there are wooden hoops of assorted sizes tied in the doorway. There is a good selection of local views (several of which appear in this book) and we are invited to enquire within for more. British and Foreign Bible Society Bibles and Testaments are available. The frontage can be compared with that on the Long Street corner at a similar date (see No 126).

137. *(Right)* Burrows the Barbers − this is one of Sherborne's lost shops. It stood in Hound Street just below Booklore, the doorway is still visible but the shop has become part of Boots the chemists. Razors were 'ground and set' and 'Ladies Combings made up' and there was a good selection of tobacco. The window seems to have been lit by electricity which was installed in Sherborne in 1923 and supplied by the generator in Westbury.

Newland

138. *(Above left)* A fine Palladian-style house once known as 'St Swithin's Laundry' by virtue of the fact that it had been purchased by the Rev E A Young 'for philanthropic purposes' who added 2 large rooms . . . 'and used the same as a model laundry'. The house stood opposite the west gate of Lord Digby's School in Newland and its foundations now lie beneath the Somerfield supermarket carpark (1990). The outer wall of the range of buildings seen to the left (east) of the house survives in the low carpark wall which leads down to the Old Market; the access road itself was created about 1960 reducing the area of Lord Digby's School tennis courts. The street line is unchanged, the present low wall fronting Newland closely follows the railings of the lost garden, although there is no longer a way through.

On the gates can be read 'Lord Digby's Secondary School for Girls' (rendered in gold paint in 1907) which occupied the house between 1898 and 1931. Subsequently it became Dewey's Garage and the ornamental garden converted into a forecourt with petrol pumps (see No 139). The house was demolished in the early 1970's – it was in a state of delapidation and felt at the time to be beyond repair. The plaster ceiling cornice from one of the principal rooms was rescued and re-mounted in the drawing room of 93 Newland. A filling station continued to operate from the site until about 1984; the area of the house itself was absorbed by Hunts Dairies.

139. *(Above right)* The old Lord Digby's School house photographed about 1950 and by then the premises of Dewey's Garage. The garden has given way to a forecourt, adjacent buildings are in use as store rooms and the garden at the rear is a parking lot for coaches and taxis. Cottages on the right were partly demolished by the Urban District Council for the stone before it was realised the buildings were listed.

140. *(Right)* The Newland frontage of Dewey's Garage as it appeared about 1950; on the extreme right the gable of the old cinema can be seen. Nothing remains of the garden railing, but a Ham Stone post can be seen to the right of the pumps. This was the site of Sherborne's first electric petrol pump.

141. *(Above)* The only recognisable feature on this photograph is the dormitory wing of Harper House in Hound Street seen in the distance. The camera is looking south across what is now the Somerfield supermarket, in fact not only before the supermarket but before the enlargement of Hunts Dairies factory which occupied this site in the 1970's. The wall behind the vehicles survives – much reduced in height – which divides the present carpark.

142. *(Above right)* The Carlton cinema in Newland was demolished in 1989 to make way for the Somerfield supermarket carpark; the archway to the right still stands. The cinema was first opened as the Wessex Theatre on 18 December 1929. It superceded the 'Picture Palace' above 59 Cheap Street (now Lancaster's) and before that films had been shown at the Rawson Hall in Westbury.

The grand opening night was, however, marred by 'technical difficulties'. It was not possible to show the film 'Hungarian Rhapsody' starring Lil Dagovar – so the town band played instead. The building was designed by a Birmingham firm, Messrs Satchwell and Roberts, and the interior was in 'old gold and oak' and handpainted hunting and pastoral scenes decorated the foyer. There was seating for 600; the Balcony cost 2s (10p) or 1/6;. Stalls, 1/2, 1/- and 6d (2½p).

The Wessex Theatre was not, however equipped for sound, and the proprietor/manager, Rowland Reeves was soon in financial difficulties. Money was put into the theatre by a Mr Carter and a Mr Pilkington who re-opened the business under the name CARLTON - a combination of the two surnames. During the 1930's the Carlton Theatre not only showed talking pictures but was the scene of successful amateur dramatic performances. The Carlton closed on 4 February 1961. The foyer became offices of Hunts Dairies, and the auditorium a vehicle maintenance shed.

143. *(Right)* The skeleton of the Carlton Cinema auditorium re-emerging during demolition work in 1988-9. Several of the red plush seats were still in situ and two are preserved in the Museum.

144. William Macready, the great Victorian actor, is standing outside Sherborne House with members of his family some time between 1850 and 1860. It was here that Macready entertained Thackeray and Dickens; the latter gave a reading of 'Marley's Ghost' in the Macready Institute next door (until recently occupied by Sherborne Youth Club). Tickets cost 3s – the price of a bad bottle of wine, remarked the *Western Gazette* reporter. But very few tickets were sold and the price reduced to 2s 6d (12½p). Macready had two sons at the King's School, Edward Neville and Walter Francis. He removed them after refusing to pay a penny fine which the Headmaster levied from the whole school to replace a badly damaged book. The younger boy died soon afterwards at the age of 14.

Sherborne House was built for Henry Seymour Portman about 1714, and Sir James Thornhill, Hogarth's father-in-law, painted the staircase murals. It has been occupied by Lord Digby's School since 1931.

145. The Manor House, Newland, photographed by John Warry of Holwell on a warm summer afternoon in 1859. There was movement while the shutter was open; the horse shook its head and a woman appeared at the cottage door beside the lamp post. The left-hand pavement is cobbled, and the road is uneven and dirty; piles of dung have been deposited by 'parked' horses (or perhaps awaiting collection by the town 'scavenger'). The origins of the Manor House are obscure, but it was certainly never a manor house. In 1735 it was described as 'late Durnford's'. The Durnford family were prominent in the town in the 17th century; between 1629 and 1684 three of them served as both governor and warden of the King's School. In 1816 the Manor House was the residence of a Mr Beale who ran goods wagons to London and by 1834 the residence of one George Warry – perhaps a relative of the photographer. By 1865 the Manor House was occupied by a school run by Mme Vantini.

146. *(Above)* The north side of Newland before the creation of North Road; the sixth house from the left (adjacent to number 67 formerly a doctors' surgery) was pulled down thus widening a small lane which had hitherto given access only to yards and gardens. The plan for North Road was passed in 1880. By 1887 the OS map shows The Manse (North Gate) Devanah ('The Bungalow'), Highlands (North Place) opposite an unnamed house, Westcott and Albert Row.

The cottages next to the Manor House were demolished in 1980 and re-built on the same site; the gardens behind were filled with the houses of Manor Court. Thus preserved was the continuous frontage of Newland which was, until the middle of the 18th century, to be found along the south side of the street. At least 6 cottages were removed to improve the view of Sherborne House, a further 2 or 3 provided the site for St Swithin's Laundry and others between Monks Barn and Hound Street, and facing the bottom of The Avenue, had gone by 1800.

147. *(Left)* Entrance to North Road; the sign reads 'THIS ROAD BLOCKED'. The width of the original lane can be seen alongside what is today 69 Newland; the foundations of the demolished house lie underneath the modern road. This development completed a through route from Coldharbour to Long Street by way of Newland (creating the site of Island House) and down the hill along what had recently become St Swithin's Road. Formerly known as Stile Close or 'Lavender Lane' (because it smelled so bad) the lane was closed in 1893 and the road created at a cost of £500.

148. *(Left)* A pair of cottages at the bottom of T[?] Avenue demolished some time before 1877, the remains of which lie beneath the middle of the present road. The railings on the left are recognisable as those of 93 Newland. The path beside the railings represents the original width o[f] what was then Coldharbour Lane, which led directly to Coldharbour, as its name suggests (the top part of the lane beside 'The Turret' has never been widened). The cottages are recorded on the town map of 1834, but not in 1733, and remains o[f] the boundary wall of their twin gardens could be seen during the building of the houses in the Littl[e] Stonegarth Garden in 1984. This garden had bee[n] created in its turn by the destruction of Miss Billinger's house, also called Stonegarth, which received a direct hit by a bomb in September 194[0]. The Avenue was taken over as a public highway o[n] 8 December 1903, but house building had begun by 1887 when the OS Map shows Semington House (Saffron Court) and Sydney Villa (Rathgar)[.]

149. *(Below)* 'Newland Park' was opened as a public space in 1896 and briefly known as 'Victoria Park'. The present plaque records the death of George VI and the coronation of Elizabeth II in June 1953. In 1967 J H P Gibb recommended to the Urban District Council that it be 'Newland Garden' which it remains. It was here the St Swithin's Fair was held; and from 1227/8 the Borough Court of Newland assembled at a market cross – the earliest reference to which is 1383/4. In 1570 a pond is depicted, and the Newland pump was one of only 6 in Sherborne in 1850. In 1735 the area was described as a 'timber yard where human bones are found, supposed site of a church or chapel'. Included in this area is the site of Island House created when St Swithin's Road was made (behind the camera). Bones were discovered while the house was under construction about 1958.

On the extreme right-hand of the picture are the two chimney stacks belonging to the old Newland Infants School.

Tinneys Lane & The Avenue

150. Newland (Foster's) Infants School at the bottom of Tinneys Lane seen on the left; members of Mrs Phillips' class are waiting on the pavement in August 1935. The school received a direct hit in the air raid of September 1940, and what remained was demolished together with two adjacent cottages. The school was founded in 1840 under the terms of the 'Green Girls Charity', some £300 was spent buying the site and erecting the school where an 'old building' had previously stood.

Tinneys Lane (Twiney Lane in 1735 meaning 'between') was a path which led out from Newland Borough to enclosed fields also called 'Newland' in 1570, an area later known as 'Field Walls' presumably in contrast to the more usual hedgerows. The end of Tinneys Lane (the site of Fosters School 1939) opened onto unenclosed arable fields worked in strips. In the late 1960's a light dusting of snow on the playing fields revealed faint traces of ridges left by medieval ploughing.

151. Horse Show about 1910 in what is now Foster's School playing fields; the houses of The Avenue can be seen in the background. The field was called 'Tinney's Lane Stall' after a cow shed, the remains of which still stand beside the road, and the adjacent field was known simply as 'Tinney's', a name adopted by the new Sherborne Youth Club opened by Prince Edward on 30 June 1990, and which now occupies the site.

152. The Avenue about 1904; the lower part of the road followed the old Coldharbour Lane, but the length in the photograph runs eastward to the camera and then north, following a hedgerow through an area formerly known as 'Field Walls' and then joining Coldharbour between fields called 'Butcher's Steps' and 'Parish Garden' the latter held in 1834 by the Parish Officers for the poor.

In the middle distance on the left is 'The Red House' built by John Carey (master at the King's School 1897-1927). Next door is 'Nortons' where Alan Turing (1912-1954) mathematician, code-breaker and 'father of the digital computer' often stayed with the Gervis family as a schoolboy. Behind the camera is 'Quarry House' built for the writer Littleton Powys by his architect brother.

In the garden of Hill House (left) a close of houses was built in 1978.

Coldharbour

153. Coldharbour looking west about 1930; perhaps the principal interest is the 'Ovaltine' poster on the hoarding! The wall on the left (which contained re-used masonry from the Old Castle) has disappeared to make way for the entrance to the new Fire Station and the building showing the poster was, in 1858, destined for greater things as 'The Terminus Hotel' at a time when it was proposed to build the railway to the north of the town (see No 109). For many years it was the 'Queen's Head'.

54. An old cottage in Coldharbour, Jack Lugg's parents are standing outside. This was certainly one of a row of Digby estate cottages shown as the only dwellings in Coldharbour in 1733, and which occupied that stretch of road between the east wall of Sherborne House (the present fire station) and the field boundary, now Wootton Grove.

The year 1884 saw a case of supposed witchcraft in Coldharbour. Old Sarah Smith, 83, who was in receipt of poor relief, was hoeing her potatoes one day when she was violently attacked by her neighbour, Mrs Tamar Humphries who, armed with a knitting needle, was intent on drawing blood from the old woman's hands and arms. Mrs Humphries told the Bench her daughter was a chronic invalid and that 'old Sal Smith' was guilty of 'witching' the girl.

55. Coldharbour looking east; the girl in the pinafore is standing outside 'Redlynch' and the next-door premises have been re-built with first floor bay window and a shop frontage and is now the 'London Road Stores'. The letter box at the top of North Road has vanished. This picture belongs to a series of post cards published before the First World War.

Coldharbour is shown as an unfenced field road about 1570 and no houses are depicted along it. It does not seem to have become a route of any importance until the days of the Turnpike Trusts and regular mailcoach services. In 1876 the plan of a Skating Rink in Coldharbour was approved, but the project was seemingly abandoned.

Cold Harbour, Sherborne.

156. The Royal Naval Hospital was built for the casualties of the Second World War – convalescents were a familiar sight in Sherborne's streets. This aerial view was taken in the 1950's looking south across Coldharbour which shows the allotments in 'Parish Garden' now part of the Castle View estate (early 1970's). After the War part of the hospital was used as a home for the mentally handicapped and in the 1960's staff accommodation was built facing Coldharbour Road. The hospital is now closed and the plan is to develop the area for housing and industry; Sherborne's new Ambulance Station is already in operation (1990).

Simons Road

157. The County Primary School in Simons Road immediately after completion in 1912; the road is still unsurfaced. The school opened on 25 July 1913 with 237 children on the roll; the headmaster was Mr C H Bacon and there were six assistant teachers.
     The houses immediately above the School (to the left) were built by Baxter's Brewery in Long Street for their workers.

158. Fox's Ice-cream Cart in Simons Road; the children seem to have posed in their best clothes! The date 1937 can just be discerned on the ice-cream container.
     Simons Road was taken over as a public highway in 1912 and the first houses date from this time. Despite considerable difficulties twenty more houses were constructed during the First World War as a town effort to provide 'homes fit for heroes'. A further twenty were built in 1923; Mr Guppy's tender of £7423 9s 0d was accepted (approximately £371 per house).

Kings Road

159. Kings Road is viewed from the Bristol Road junction looking east to Wootton Grove some time in the early years of the century. Along both sides of a wide straight carriageway, and behind enclosed front gardens, are ranged the imposing facades of privately-built Edwardian villas, making Kings Road among the first of Sherborne's wholly 'residential' roads. The king we suggest, is Edward VII.

160. Irene Moores runs through the gate of 'Halstock', King's Road, in the summer of either 1907 or 1908. The low brick wall and the ornate ironwork are still in existence. As yet there is no house opposite, giving a clear view of the site of the Grove Health Centre which opened in January 1990. The houses of Wootton Grove are already well established, but King's Road is still under construction; it was not taken over as a public highway until 1914. In the centre of the picture is a haystack, last reminder of a lost field, the boundary of which had been closely followed in the course of the new road.